Hearing the Word of God

Hearing the Word of God

Reflections on the Sunday Readings
Year B

John R. Donahue, S.J.

THE LITURGICAL PRESS
Collegeville, Minnesota

www.litpress.org

Contents

Calendar for 2002–2003

Introduction   ix

First Sunday of Advent   1

Second Sunday of Advent   4

Third Sunday of Advent   6

Fourth Sunday of Advent   9

A Yuletide Medley   11

    The Nativity of the Lord   11

    The Holy Family of Jesus, Mary, and Joseph   13

    Solemnity of the Blessed Virgin Mary, the Mother of God   15

    The Epiphany of the Lord   17

The Baptism of the Lord   19

Second Sunday in Ordinary Time   21

Third Sunday in Ordinary Time   23

The Presentation of the Lord   25

Fifth Sunday in Ordinary Time   28

Sixth Sunday in Ordinary Time   30

Seventh Sunday in Ordinary Time   32

Eighth Sunday in Ordinary Time   35

Ash Wednesday   38

First Sunday of Lent   40

Second Sunday of Lent   43

Third Sunday of Lent   46

Fourth Sunday of Lent   49

Fifth Sunday of Lent   52

Palm Sunday of the Lord's Passion   55

Easter Sunday   58

Second Sunday of Easter   61

Third Sunday of Easter   64

Fourth Sunday of Easter   67

Fifth Sunday of Easter   70

Sixth Sunday of Easter   73

The Ascension of the Lord   75

Seventh Sunday of Easter   77

Pentecost Sunday   80

The Solemnity of the Most Holy Trinity   82

The Solemnity of the Most Holy Body and Blood of Christ   84

SS. Peter and Paul, Apostles   86

Fourteenth Sunday in Ordinary Time   89

Fifteenth Sunday in Ordinary Time   91

Sixteenth Sunday in Ordinary Time   93

Seventeenth Sunday in Ordinary Time   95

Eighteenth Sunday in Ordinary Time   97

Nineteenth Sunday in Ordinary Time   100

Twentieth Sunday in Ordinary Time   102

Twenty-First Sunday in Ordinary Time   104

Twenty-Second Sunday in Ordinary Time   106

Twenty-Third Sunday in Ordinary Time   108

The Exaltation of the Holy Cross   110

Twenty-Fifth Sunday in Ordinary Time   113

Twenty-Sixth Sunday in Ordinary Time   116

Twenty-Seventh Sunday in Ordinary Time   119

Twenty-Eighth Sunday in Ordinary Time   121

Twenty-Ninth Sunday in Ordinary Time   124

Thirtieth Sunday in Ordinary Time   127

Commemoration of All the Faithful Departed (All Souls)   129

The Dedication of the Lateran Basilica   132

Thirty-Third Sunday in Ordinary Time   135

The Solemnity of Our Lord Jesus Christ the King   138

Appendix

The following Sundays do not occur in 2002–2003 but are included here for possible use in a future year that uses Cycle B. The feasts of the Transfiguration and All Saints are not transferred to Sunday.

Fourth Sunday in Ordinary Time   142

Ninth Sunday in Ordinary Time   144

Tenth Sunday in Ordinary Time   146

Eleventh Sunday in Ordinary Time   149

Twelfth Sunday in Ordinary Time   152

Thirteenth Sunday in Ordinary Time   155

The Transfiguration of the Lord (August 6)   157

Twenty-Fourth Sunday in Ordinary Time   159

All Saints   162

Thirty-First Sunday in Ordinary Time   164

Thirty-Second Sunday in Ordinary Time   167

Introduction

When the bishops of the Second Vatican Council entered St. Peter's Basilica in solemn procession behind an ancient manuscript of the Scriptures and conducted their deliberations before it enshrined in a place of honor, they were enacting a parable of the role of Scripture in the council itself and in the postconciliar Church. The Church is summoned to be a follower and servant of the Word. The major document on Scripture issued by the council, the Dogmatic Constitution on Divine Revelation *(Dei Verbum)*, begins with the phrase "Hearing the Word of God with reverence, and proclaiming it with faith," and in the documents on bishops and priests, proclamation and exposition of the Word are listed first among their ministries. Most importantly, the Bible was given back to the people. Biblical study not only was to be the soul of theology but was to inform all aspects of Church life.

I remember a conversation I had shortly after Vatican II with Fr. R. A. F. MacKenzie, S.J., one of the great pioneers in modern Catholic biblical study. He felt that the renewal of Scripture by the council would be its most lasting and significant contribution. During the four decades since the council, the Catholic community has been transformed into a Bible-reading, Bible-praying Church that continues to attract new or renewed members through biblical-based programs such as the Rite of Christian Initiation of Adults (RCIA). Over the past thirty years, from Anaheim to Zimbabwe, I have given over three hundred lectures on Scripture in different settings—Scripture institutes, study weeks, individual lectures—and can testify to the hunger of people for the exposition of Scripture. Personally I have been nurtured and encouraged by the kinds of questions people raise and by their dedication and love of Scripture.

The Catholic community has produced a wealth of resources ranging from scholarly commentaries to parish study programs, and The Liturgical Press has been a leader in making such resources available. The present reflections first appeared as "The Word" column in the national Jesuit weekly *America,* covering Cycle B, from November 20, 1999, to November 18, 2000. Since some Sundays in the cycle were displaced by particular feasts, reflections on these Sundays have been added.

My purpose in the reflections was not to offer careful exegetical comments on each reading nor to suggest direct topics for preaching. Usually I focused on the gospel in its liturgical context and attempted to offer a few ideas or perspectives that could be used in preaching or in personal prayer and reflection. The greatest compliment a writer can receive is to find that someone has taken a suggestion and developed it in his or her own way or has been stimulated to insights that I as an author did not have. Naturally there are time-conditioned references in the various reflections, and these have not been altered, even though now they may have a more historical than actual significance.

I am most grateful to Fr. Thomas Reese, s.j., the editor of *America*, who invited me to do the original columns, and especially to Fr. Robert Collins, s.j. the managing editor, who read each column carefully and suggested changes and corrections. Very special thanks go to Ms. Toni Tortorilla, a recent and distinguished graduate of the Master of Divinity program at the Jesuit School of Theology at Berkeley, who did the lion's share of editing the final manuscript with dedication and care. I am also grateful to the editors of The Liturgical Press for accepting and preparing the final version.

JOHN R. DONAHUE, s.j.

Raymond E. Brown Distinguished Professor of New Testament Studies
St. Mary's Seminary and University, Baltimore, Maryland

First Sunday of Advent

Readings: Isa 63:16b-17, 19b; 64:2-7; Ps 80:2-3, 15-16, 18-19;
1 Cor 1:3-9; Mark 13:33-37

"Be watchful! Be alert! You do not know
when the time will come" (Mark 13:33).

LEARNING TO TELL TIME

The Advent readings, which initiate a new Church year, provide a polyphonous chorus of themes and motifs. Expectation of the various "comings" of Christ dominate: the coming in history, which culminates the four weeks of preparation; his coming at the end of history, which is highlighted by the liturgical readings that conclude the Church year and provide a transition to the First Sunday of Advent; and his continual coming by faith into the lives of believers. The readings range from the elegant poetry of Isaiah to the strident calls for repentance of John the Baptist. It is a time of eager expectation and of absence and longing when, after today's gospel, even the voice of Jesus is silent. The readings for this first Sunday summon Christians to wait in faithful hope and to be vigilant and alert, for God may touch their lives in surprising ways.

The collage of texts from Third Isaiah (Isaiah 56–66) captures the yearning of the returning Babylonian exiles for a renewed experience of God. They remember a God who "wrought awesome deeds we could not hope for" (Isa 64:2), evoking the memories of the first exodus from Egypt and the return to the land as a renewed exodus from slavery. Yet they live between the times—the time of return and of restoration of worship in a rebuilt Temple. The experience of exile has deepened their sense of the sovereignty and centrality of God, which transcend ethnic and national identity:

> Were Abraham not to know us,
> nor Israel to acknowledge us,
> You, LORD, are our father (Isa 63:16).

1

Recalling the challenge of the prophets, they pray that "you would meet us doing justice"(NAB: "doing right"; Isa 64:4).

Today's gospel is from the end of Mark's apocalyptic discourse (ch. 13), in which Jesus predicts the destruction of the Temple, the persecutions that await the community, the arrival of "false messiahs, and false prophets"and the final cosmic catastrophes that herald the return of the Son of Man to gather the elect. This conclusion presents a short parable that is bracketed by three commands to Jesus' followers, "Be watchful"(13:33, 35, 37), because they do not know the proper time *(kairos)* for God to intervene. It is a virtual allegory of the community life of Mark's small house churches, which compares Jesus' absence to a journey by the head of the house, who has delegated authority to servants. Each has a different task, with a special commission to the doorkeeper to be watchful, for the "lord"may return at one of the four watches of the night (evening, middle of the night, cockcrow, or morning). It is a community yearning for the return of Jesus and for visible signs of God's presence.

This parable also anticipates the passion of Jesus (Mark 14–16). Jesus' final hours are punctuated by the same four watches, and ironically the disciples fail to watch in Gethsemane (14:32-44), Peter denies him at cockcrow (14:72), and Pilate condemns him in the morning (15:1-15). Rather paradoxically, while waiting for Jesus to return in power and glory as the exalted Son of Man (13:26-27), the disciples fail to see his coming as the suffering Son of Man, who gives his life that others may be free (10:45)—a warning to contemporary Christians preoccupied with the "Second Coming."

These readings provide multiple challenges to Christians today, especially during the often hectic weeks before Christmas, in which waiting suggests endless traffic jams or long lines while shopping for that special gift, and watching is scarcely the vigilance that Mark calls for but often means staring at a cavalcade of Christmas television specials or seemingly never-ending athletic events. Biblical watching consists of faithful waiting and attentiveness to the *kairos* of God's entry into our diverse individual and corporate histories. It is for us, as for Mark's community, enduring hope and fidelity to the tasks of our lives in the face of God's absence. For us, as for the returning exiles, faithful waiting unfolds between memory of God's awesome deeds and yearning for a God who can accomplish what no eye has seen nor ear has heard "for those who wait."

PRAYING WITH SCRIPTURE

- In this hectic season, seek out moments of quiet and recall those awesome deeds of God that have touched your life.

- What are some ways that you yearn for the surprising presence of Christ in your life?

- Can we, like the returning exiles, seek a God who transcends our national and religious heritage and who will meet us doing justice?

Second Sunday of Advent

Readings: Isa 40:1-5, 9-11; Ps 85:9-14; 2 Pet 3:8-14; Mark 1:1-8

**"Justice shall walk before him,
and prepare the way of his steps" (Ps 85:14).**

THINK AGAIN

Last Sunday the readings echoed with expectation for the coming of Christ at the end of history. Today they speak of beginnings. The Old Testament reading, now enshrined among the sounds of Advent as the opening recitative of Handel's *Messiah*, "Comfort ye, Comfort ye, my people," inaugurates the Book of Consolation (Isaiah 40–56). The voice of God cries out in the wilderness (NAB: "wasteland") to the exiles in Babylon that their "service is at an end" and their "guilt is expiated" (Isa 40:2).

The opening verses of the Gospel of Mark reach back to Isaiah (and to Exod 23:29; Mal 3:1) to hear again a voice in the wilderness calling the people to make way for the coming of God (Isa 40:3; 42:16). By "beginning" (1:1) Mark means not simply the initial verses of a book but the origin or foundation of the Church's proclamation of the Good News (13:10; 14:9) in the deepest aspirations of the Jewish people for liberation and intimacy with God (Isaiah) and in the life, death, and raising up of Jesus. These verses also provide an overture to Mark's story of Jesus by sounding those themes that resonate throughout his text: "the way" as a metaphor for the path of discipleship (8:27; 9:33-34; 10:52; 12:14); Jesus, Messiah (8:29; 14:61; 15:32) and Son of God (3:11; 5:7; 14:61; 15:39); proclaiming the Good News (1:14; 3:14; 13:10); forgiveness of sin (2:1-12; 3:28; 11:25); the coming of the stronger one (1:22, 27; 3:20-27).

Mark introduces the second of the three Advent figures of expectation (Isaiah, John the Baptist, and Mary). In this year's cycle of Lectionary readings, John is at center stage also next Sunday. John's location in the desert, the barren wilderness southeast of Jerusalem near the Dead Sea, has broad resonance for Jews, recalling the years of wilderness wandering between the Exodus and the entry into the land, and the place of the covenant at Sinai (Exod 19–24). It has a dual connotation: positively, of the place of God's saving acts and betrothal with the people (Jer 2:2-3; Hos 2:14-15; Ps 78:12-53; Ps 105:39-45); and negatively, of the site of testing and rebellion (Exod 16; Num 11; Ps 78:17-22, 32-41; Ps 106:6-43). Jesus is tested there in Mark 1:12-13, retreats there to pray (1:35) and to avoid crowds (1:45), and there feeds the people (6:31-32). His final test comes when he is "deserted" by his followers and accepts the chalice of suffering (Mark 14:32-50).

Today John, the wild, ascetic prophet, summons people to a baptism of repentance, a symbolic washing that signals a new way of thinking. "Repentance," with its overtones of sorrow, contrition, and "purpose of amendment," disguises the rich nuance of the Greek *metanoia*, which rather suggests a "second look," "taking stock," "recollection and renewal." Such repentance leads to forgiveness (literally: "sending away") of sin with overtones of pardon, release from captivity, and cancellation of punishment. Jesus himself will leave the desert to begin his ministry by joining a call for *metanoia* to the joyful proclamation of the Good News and of the nearness of God's reign (Mark 1:14-15).

The reading from Isaiah and the gospel offer different opportunities for contemporary preaching and appropriation: the rooting of Christian faith in the Jewish Scriptures; a paradoxical warrior-God who rules "by his strong arm" (Isa 40:10) but comes with power to lead exiles home and feed his flock like a shepherd; joy over the good news of a God "who proclaims peace to his people" (Ps 85:9); the ambivalence of the "desert" (not simply literally but of times of our lives) as the place of testing and failure but also of renewed love; the presentation of Jesus as the stronger one in a contemporary world that seems fragile and threatening; the need in Advent to take "a second look" at our lives; reflection on the different paths that lie before us; a longing for "a new heaven and a new earth where the justice of God will reside" (2 Pet 3:13; au. trans.).

PRAYING WITH SCRIPTURE

- Stand in the desert among the crowds and listen again to John's words: "think again," "take stock," "prepare the way of God."

- Can Advent and Christmas be a celebration in our lives and churches of return and homecoming by a God who gathers in exiles?

- Where is the good news of "new beginnings" to be found today?

Third Sunday of Advent

Readings: Isa 61:1-2a, 10-11; (Resp.) Luke 1:46-50, 53-54;
1 Thess 5:16-24; John 1:6-8, 19-28

"My spirit rejoices in God my Savior" (Luke 1:47).

ARE YOU A PROPHET?

The Lectionary offers a panoply of readings dictated by liturgical concerns, especially joy over the approaching messianic age, crystallized by Paul's advice to the Thessalonians: "Rejoice always. Pray without ceasing. In all circumstances give thanks" (1 Thess 5:16-18). In the first reading, from Isaiah, a messianic (anointed) figure announces glad tidings that touch all aspects of life, good news to the lowly, healing and liberation, a year of jubilee and a harvest of justice. The song following the first reading for this Sunday, one of the very rare occasions when the Lectionary does not prescribe a psalm, is from Mary's *Magnificat*, with its refrain of joy over the mighty things God has done for and through her.

The gospel again brings John the Baptist to the forefront, but now heavily influenced by the theology of the Fourth Gospel, which considerably changes his role. He is not the Messiah, nor Elijah preceding the Messiah (Mark 9:9-13), nor even a prophet. His baptism is not for repentance, but simply water baptism. In John's theology, John the Baptist is primarily a witness to the light (1:8, also 3:28-29; 5:31-35). Since Jesus' whole life, in the Gospel of John, is a trial by his own who did not receive him (1:10-11) and by a hostile world (7:7), *witness* takes on the legal nuance of truthful and courageous testimony about Jesus. Other witnesses are Jesus himself, the works of Jesus and the Father (5:36-37), the Samaritan woman (4:39), the Paraclete and the disciples (15:26-27).

An Advent theme first sounded last week in the responsorial psalm, "justice and peace shall kiss" (Ps 85:11), and reverberating through the third Sunday is God' s justice, which is expressed in concern for the poor and oppressed. Isaiah announces a year of the Lord's favor, a jubilee. Mary speaks as a prophet of justice taking the side of the suffering people and threatening the rich. "Biblical justice" is different from contemporary legal understandings of justice. It conveys a sense of things being "right" and is one of the prime covenant qualities, intimately linked with other fundamental dispositions: "I will espouse you in right and in justice; in love and in mercy; I will espouse you in fidelity" (Hos 2:21-22). Justice is to be enacted by the king, safeguarded by the prophet, and lived by God's people.

Biblical justice is fidelity to the demands of a relationship and involves a call to be in right relationship to God and neighbor. Nor is it totally neutral; it is partial to those most in need. The symbol of biblical justice is not a blindfolded woman with scales in her hand but another woman, Mary of Nazareth, heralding a God who scatters the proud in their hearts, brings down the powerful from their thrones, fills the hungry with good things, and sends the rich away empty (Luke 1:51-52).

Advent of 1999 ushered in what Pope John Paul II called the Great Jubilee. In announcing the jubilee, the Pope turned to Isaiah 61:1-10 (repeated in Luke 4:18-19) and called on the Church to celebrate the jubilee by being in right relationship with God and neighbor through personal conversion, repentance over individual and corporate sinfulness, and reconciliation with enemies (apostolic letter *Tertio Millenio Adveniente*, Nov. 10, 1994). He also stressed the social dimension of this jubilee: "From this point of view, if we recall that Jesus came to 'preach the good news to the poor' (Matt 11:5; Luke 7:22), how can we fail to lay greater emphasis on the Church's preferential option for the poor and the outcast? Indeed, it has to be said that a commitment to justice and peace in a world like ours, marked by so many conflicts and intolerable social and economic inequalities, is a necessary condition for the preparation and celebration of the Jubilee." No justice, no jubilee!

The readings this Sunday provide rich options for preaching and reflection: a God partial to the lowly, the brokenhearted and captives; joy over the nearness of God's anointed; the summons to be courageous witnesses whose lives are eloquent testimony to the advent of God's incarnate Word; the challenge, even amid the din of a busy and commercialized season, to open our hearts and ears to the call of Pope John Paul II for a commitment to peace and justice, and to the voice of Mary confronting the proud and the powerful and speaking for those who have no voice.

Praying with Scripture

- Think of people, times, or events that have brought forth true joy in your life and render constant thanks (1 Thess 5:16).

- What testimony is most needed by the Church today? How can Catholics be witnesses to the presence of Christ?

- How does God call us to manifest a commitment to peace and justice in a world "marked by so many conflicts and intolerable social and economic inequalities" (Pope John Paul II)?

Fourth Sunday of Advent

Readings: 2 Sam 7:1-5, 8b-12, 14a, 16; Ps 89:2-5, 27, 29;
Rom 16:25-27; Luke 1:26-38

"The power of the Most High will overshadow you" (Luke 1:35).

RESPONSE AND GIFT

As Advent draws to a close, Mary, the third figure of expectation, oc-
cupies center stage. Today's Gospel also provides a transition and introduction to the Christmas cycle, which extends to Epiphany. Apart
from Epiphany and one Christmas Mass, the readings are taken from
Luke's carefully composed infancy narratives, which also foreshadow
the major themes of his Gospel and Acts: Jesus, Savior and Messiah
(2:11); his prophetic mission (2:31-35); the outpouring of God's spirit
(1:15, 35, 41, 67); joy over God's actions (1:14, 44, 47; 2:1); the presence
and importance of women in God's saving action (1:27-55; 2:22-52);
God's concern for the poor and the marginal (1:52-53); and the forgiveness of sin (1:77). Luke arranges these narratives around two diptychs
of John and Jesus, each comprising two narratives of annunciation and
conception, and of birth, naming, and promise of future greatness.

This careful composition and theological density are in tension with
the Lectionary's use of Luke 1 and 2, since sections are excerpted, often
out of context. True appropriation and proclamation of these gospels
requires attention to the gospel context as well as to liturgical use. It is
important to read and proclaim the gospel reading on a given Sunday
in the context of the complete Gospel by a particular evangelist.

Luke's annunciation narrative follows a pattern: appearance of an
angel, fear, message, objection, and confirmatory sign of God's presence. This reflects Old Testament birth announcements (Gen 16:7-12;
17:1-20; Judg 13:3-21) and prophetic calls (Isa 6:1-13; Jer 1:4-19). Two
themes shape this narrative: the focus on Jesus as Son of the Most High

9

and heir to the throne of David (first reading), and the role of Mary, which has so captured Christian art and imagination through the ages. Though told as a parallel to the announcement of John's birth, the birth of Jesus is accentuated by Luke. Mary is greeted as "most favored," ("full of grace"), that is, the recipient of God's special love; she is a virgin and the Holy Spirit will overshadow her. She alone will give Jesus a name and destiny, and her consent opens the way for the coming of the child called the holy one and Son of God.

Mary is a model of expectation for the contemporary Church. She is a "handmaid" *(doulē),* a term liable to misintepretation as encouraging passivity. But the term is used frequently to describe significant figures in salvation history (Moses at Exod 4:10; 14:31; Num 12:7; Deut 34:5; David at 2 Sam 7:5; and Isaiah at Isa 20:3) and becomes a frequent self-designation by the apostle Paul (e.g., Rom 1:1; 2 Cor 4:5; Phil 1:1). The prophetic role of Mary is lost sight of in the seasonal Lectionary, since the *Magnificat*, which follows the annunciation, appears as a Gospel reading only on the feast of the Assumption.

At the annunciation, Mary is one who, like Moses, stands in awe of God's presence; like the prophets, she accepts a commission from God and lives out of faith in God's word ("May it be done to me according to your word"). The Church, through the ages and today, is sustained by women and men who experience the overshadowing power of God's spirit, live in prophetic service of God's word, and bring forth God's presence in the world.

PRAYING WITH SCRIPTURE

• During this season read meditatively Luke 1 and 2, placing yourself in the scene, identifying with different characters, and asking how their stories touch your life today.

A Yuletide Medley

December 25
The Nativity of the Lord

Readings: Isa 9:1-6; Ps 96:1-3, 11-13; Titus 2:11-14; Luke 2:1-14

**"Do not be afraid; for behold, I proclaim
to you good news of great joy" (Luke 2:10).**

A GIFT THAT IS NEVER RETURNED

Because of the ancient custom of celebrating three distinct Christmas Masses, the liturgy offers a treasury of readings that bring out different aspects of the celebration. The first readings herald the messianic promises of Isaiah and the good news of salvation (Isa 57:7-10; 62:11-12), and the psalms echo Israel's royal enthronement rituals. The gospels for the Masses at midnight and morning announce in rhythmic cadence Luke's story of the birth and initial revelation of Jesus, while John's poetic prologue (John 1:1-18, the gospel for Mass during the day), reaches beyond time to proclaim that the Word that was with God and was God has become flesh and made his dwelling place among us.

Taken together, these gospels offer diverse perspectives on the mystery of the Incarnation. Luke's account is filled with paradox. Jesus' birth takes place during the reign of Caesar Augustus (27 B.C. to A.D. 14), who rules over "the whole world" and was known for bringing peace after years of civil strife. An ancient inscription celebrates the birthday of Augustus as "good news for the whole world." Yet Jesus, whose parents are from the little-known town of Nazareth on the fringe of Augustus's empire, and who is laid in a manger, is Messiah and Lord and will bring peace to those "on whom his favor rests" (Luke 2:14). His birth is not announced in city squares throughout the empire but to shepherds, a group often scorned by the religious elite of the day.

The beauty of Luke's narrative and its influence on Christian art, literature, and music remind us that through the Incarnation, the human condition is now suffused with God's beauty. Still, the contemporary marketing of Christmas can mask the stark reality of Jesus' birth. St. Ignatius instructs us in his Spiritual Exercises that when contemplating the Nativity, we are to see how the persons in the scene are laboring so that "Jesus may be born in greatest poverty; and that after so many hardships of hunger, thirst, heat, cold, injuries, and insults, he may die on the cross." Luke may be hinting at this by his use of the same term for the "inn" (Luke 2:7) that did not welcome Mary and Joseph and for the "guest room" (Luke 22:11, *katalyma*) where Jesus celebrates his final supper and speaks of his body, which will be given "for you" and his blood shed "for you." The shadow of the cross falls even upon the crèche of Bethlehem.

Taken together, Luke's narrative and John's hymn (1:1-18) emphasize the paradox of Christian faith in the Incarnation: truly human, truly divine; eternal Word, a life unfolding in history. This paradox is also a tension. The "high Christology" of John can envelop the human Jesus; neglect of the transcendent Word made flesh can reduce Jesus to a compassionate social prophet or innocent martyr. There is another paradox. When Christians gather to pray at Christmas, they must recall that Jesus' life and death are not only "for us" but through the Word now incarnate "was life, and this life was the light of the human race" (John 1:4). The human condition has been radically changed by the coming of Christ, and this is cause for "good news of great joy."

PRAYING WITH SCRIPTURE

- When looking at the Christmas crib, pray for those many families made homeless by poverty and war. Ask what gift we as Christians can give them.

- Amid the busyness of Christmas day, pause in prayer to think of those gifts of God that you most treasure.

Sunday Within the Octave of Christmas

The Holy Family of Jesus, Mary, and Joseph

Readings: Sir 3:2-6, 12-14; Ps 128:1-5; Col 3:12-17 [21]; Luke 2:22-40

"The child's father and mother were amazed at what was said about him" (Luke 2:33).

Waiting in Hope

The tone for the feast of the Holy Family is set immediately by the reading from Sirach, a collection of religious instructions guiding individuals, families, and the community in their daily lives. The "duties toward parents" follow "duties toward God." The call for love and reverence toward mother and father, and especially for the aging parent, is as topical as at first writing (ca. 180 B.C.).

The optional shorter reading from Colossians (3:12-17) omits the time-conditioned advice that wives be submissive to their husbands and focuses on those virtues which should characterize all Christian life and which are first taught in a loving family: compassion, gentleness, humility, patience, mutual forgiveness. Over these, to be worn like an outer garment, is love. Christians are summoned to remember their baptism, when they clothed themselves with Christ (Gal 3:27), and today might think of the wedding finery as a symbol of a new clothing in the Pauline virtues.

To capture the true spirit of the feast, read the whole of Luke 2:22-40 rather than the permitted truncated version (Luke 2:22, 39-40). The narrative begins with Mary and Joseph, in fidelity to the Law of Moses, consecrating their first born son, Jesus, "to the Lord" (Exod 13:2, 12) with a symbolic offering of two turtledoves or young pigeons, which were given by those too poor to offer a lamb (Lev 12:1-8).

Luke's main focus is on Simeon and Anna, a just couple who were waiting in hope for the Messiah. After taking the child in his arms, Simeon prays the memorable *Nunc Dimittis*, "Now, Master, you may let your servant go in peace," as he predicts that this child will be "a light for revelation to the Gentiles, and glory for your people Israel." In more somber terms he then turns to Mary and predicts that her son will be a sign that is contradicted and that a sword will pierce her. This is not, as is often thought, a reference to Mary at the foot of the cross, since she is there only in John's Gospel, but to the "sword which divides," (cf. Heb 4:12). Mary's initial yes is challenged and deepened as her son's life unfolds.

The presence of the eighty-four-year-old prophetess Anna, a widow who had spent most of her life in prayer and fasting, concludes the narrative. She gives thanks and "spoke about the child to all who were awaiting the redemption of Jerusalem." Luke's infancy narrative ends at this point with Anna, like Mary (Luke 1:46-55), thanking God and speaking of the destiny of Jesus—the young virgin mother and the elderly widow united in bringing forth God's Word to the waiting world.

PRAYING WITH SCRIPTURE

- Pray in thanksgiving for those of the older generation who have handed on faith and hope to people today.

- Pray especially for graces that you think would benefit your family.

Solemnity of the Blessed Virgin Mary, the Mother of God

Readings: Num 6:22-27; Ps 67:2-3, 5, 6, 8; Gal 4:4-7; Luke 2:16-21

"The LORD look upon you kindly and give you peace!"
(Num 6:26).

BRINGING FORTH IN FAITH

This feast has different levels: circumcision and naming of Jesus; blessing on the New Year; and since 1969, praise of Mary as *Theotokos,* Mother of God. The readings capture these different dimensions. The priestly blessing from Numbers fits the hope for a new year (and millennium) when God will be gracious, look upon us kindly, and grant us peace, while the second reading underscores the theological focus of Mary as mother of God's Son, "born of a woman, born under the law," as well as the call of Christians to be sons and daughters of God (Gal 4:7).

On the narrative level the gospel seems out of place, since it precedes the gospel for the Holy Family and returns to the early days of Jesus' life with the visit of the shepherds and the circumcision and naming of Jesus. Jesus' circumcision, the sign of the covenant, continues the theme of his solidarity with Judaism. The naming of Jesus is meant to recall the Annunciation and the promise of future greatness.

While honoring Mary on this day as Mother of God, we might recall that during the Second Vatican Council, Pope Paul VI called her Mother of the Church. Mary is also a model of the Church as mother. Long ago St. Ambrose exhorted his congregation: "Let Mary's soul be in each of you to proclaim the greatness of the Lord. Let her spirit be in each to rejoice in the Lord. Christ has only one mother in the flesh, but we all bring forth Christ in faith" (Liturgy of the Hours for December 21,

Office of Readings). On this octave of Christmas all Christians must remember that they, too, have conceived Christ in their hearts and are called to bring him forth to a suffering world.

PRAYING WITH SCRIPTURE (after the feast of Epiphany)

- The gospel speaks of Mary keeping in her heart and reflecting on the meaning of Jesus' birth. Prayerfully imitate her actions.

- St. Paul says that by God's spirit we are adopted into the very family of God. Pray especially for those people who adopt children into their families.

Sunday Between January 2 and January 8

The Epiphany of the Lord

Readings: Isa 60:1-6; Ps. 72:1-2, 7-8, 10-13; Eph 3:2-3a, 5-6; Matt 2:1-12

"Then you shall be radiant at what you see" (Isa 60:5).

JOY FOR ALL PEOPLES

The Epiphany, or showing forth, of the "newborn king of the Jews" (Isa 2:2) to magi, learned sages from the East, is celebrated by the Eastern Churches as *the* remembrance of the gift of the Incarnation for all peoples. The readings resound with themes of universality. The excerpt from Third Isaiah (first reading) expresses the hope of the pilgrimage of the nations to the one God of Israel, and the author of Ephesians, who had earlier spoken of Christ breaking down the wall of enmity between Jew and Gentile (Eph 2:14), speaks of both groups as "coheirs, members of the same body, and copartners in the promise in Christ Jesus through the gospel" (Eph 3:6).

Matthew's main focus is the universal benefits of the Messiah's advent. The visit of Gentiles (nations) at the birth anchors an arch over the whole Gospel, which ends with the risen Jesus commissioning his disciples to make disciples of "all nations" (Matt 28:19). As "Gentiles," they receive their revelation through natural creation—a symbol of the innate quest for God (see Acts 17:22-31; Rom 1:19-20). Matthew's night visitors are developed in Christian art and literature. They become three kings, and later one becomes a person of color. The bounds of inclusiveness are extended. As the Church becomes a world culture, one of its major challenges will be to be inclusive, to welcome "the other," and to break down various destructive walls of hostility—ethnic, religious, national, and socio-economic.

PRAYING WITH SCRIPTURE

As the Christmas season draws to a close, in contemplation and quiet recall the themes of the different readings.

- The gift and presence of God manifest in the coming of Christ and the surprising ways God enters human life.

- The welcome to this gift by the marginal in the world's eyes: a priest of minor rank and his wife longing for a child; a young mother from a poor village; shepherds going about their ordinary work; an aging man and woman waiting in hope and fidelity.

- The values of the gospel that challenge us today: weakness vs. power; peace vs. violence; care for others vs. autonomy; openness to the presence of God among "the other" vs. limited perspectives.

- The universality of the Church and the way it is continually enriched by people of different cultures.

Sunday After Epiphany

The Baptism of the Lord

(First Sunday in Ordinary Time)

Readings: Isa 42:1-4, 6-7; Ps 29:1-4, 9-10; Acts 10:34-38; Mark 1:7-11
Optional: Isa 55:1-11; Resp. Isa 12:2-6; 1 John 5:1-9

**"Here is my servant whom I uphold,
my chosen one with whom I am pleased" (Isa 42:1).**

HEAVENLY VOICE, EARTHLY MISSION

The feast of the Baptism of the Lord concludes the Advent-Christmas liturgical season and is also the first Sunday in Ordinary Time. In the early Church it was closely linked to Epiphany as a "manifestation" of the Son of God. This first appearance of Jesus is marked by the solemn biblical formula "It came to pass" (see Luke 1:4; 2:1), which links the baptism to significant beginnings in salvation history. The baptism also marks the advent of the "mightier" one (Mark 1:7), who submits to John's baptism of repentance in solidarity with the sinful human condition (see 2 Cor 5:21).

The focus of the narrative is on the rending of the heavens, the descent of the Spirit, and the heavenly voice pronouncing Jesus as "my beloved Son; with whom I am well pleased." In the ancient cosmology, the tearing open of the heavens would symbolize the possibility of divine-human communication (Ezek 1:1; John 1:51; Rev 19:11). It is also an eschatological motif (see Isa 24:17-20; 64:1: "Oh, that you would rend the heavens and come down") and foreshadows the "rending" of the Temple veil at the death of Jesus. These words of divine acceptance reflect different Old Testament texts: Ps 2:7, a psalm of royal adoption; Isa 42:1-2, the first of four Servant Songs from Second Isaiah. It describes a servant chosen by God, "with whom I am pleased," / "upon whom I have put my spirit." Since Mark uses frequently the literary

19

technique of foreshadowing, the heavenly declaration anticipates the voice at the Transfiguration in Mark 9:7: "This is my beloved Son." Jesus' baptism also foreshadows that "baptism" when he will be drenched in suffering, and will also be the destiny of those who would follow him. The gift of the Spirit and heavenly voice are simultaneously a prophetic commission to Jesus (see Isa 11:2; 61:1; 63:9), which will unfold throughout the Gospel, as he himself confronts the mystery of suffering and death.

This narrative provided the Markan community an opportunity not simply to understand Jesus but also to reflect on their own baptism. By God's gift of faith they moved from change of heart (Mark 1:14) to baptism, and, in Pauline terms, became God's adopted sons and daughters through the gift of the Spirit. This feast challenges Christians today to reflect on their own baptism as the gift of the Spirit and as a commission to live and proclaim the good news amid the paradox of following the "mightier" One even to the powerlessness of the cross.

Praying with Scripture

- Recall those times when you have experienced in a special way the sense of call and mission: a child's baptism; your own baptism; marriage; religious profession; ordination; acceptance of a special call.

- Pray in gratitude for those people who helped you in your journey of faith and deeper entry into the mystery of Christ.

- How are these readings a "wake-up" call for your baptismal vocation to bring others to Christ?

Second Sunday in Ordinary Time

*Readings: 1 Sam 3:3-10, 19; Ps 40:2, 4, 7-10; 1 Cor 6:13-15a, 17-20;
John 1:35-42*

"What are you looking for?" (John 1:38).

SEEK AND YOU SHALL BE FOUND

The liturgical year involves the festal cycle comprising Advent-Christmas and Lent-Paschaltide, and Ordinary Time, which is the weekly celebration of the extraordinary event of the proclamation of the word and the eucharistic paschal mystery. After the feast of the Baptism of the Lord, the readings of the second and third Sundays of this time focus on discipleship, a sign that our "ordinary" lives unfold as a following of Christ.

The theme of call and response permeates the readings. Samuel, who was to be the great prophet who anointed David, receives a threefold call while sleeping (an encouraging note to preacher and people on a gray mid-January Sunday) and finally responds: "Speak, LORD, for your servant is listening." The Lectionary unfortunately omits 1 Samuel 3:11, where Samuel hears from God: "I am about to do something in Israel that will cause the ears of everyone who hears it to ring." God is literally commissioning a "wake-up" call to the people.

The gospel from John depicts the call and response of Jesus' first followers as part of a series of initial revelations of Jesus that culminate at the wedding feast at Cana where Jesus "revealed his glory, and his disciples began to believe in him" (John 2:11). The "calls" reflect distinctive Johannine themes. John is a witness who points out Jesus as the "Lamb of God, who takes away the sin of the world" (John 1:29), evoking the Suffering Servant of Isaiah 53:5-12 and the sacrifice of the paschal lamb. The two disciples follow Jesus, but, unlike the Synoptics, Jesus asks, "What are you looking for?" They respond "Rabbi" (an inadequate answer), but Jesus invites them to stay (abide) with him (John

1:38-39). The next day Andrew finds his brother Simon and tells him, "We have found the Messiah" (John 1:41) and brings him to Jesus, from whom he receives the name Cephas (Peter).

This narrative is a Johannine "coming to faith" story not only for John's original readers but for Christians today. The questions and commands highlight the process: "What are you looking for?" "Where are you staying?" "Come, and you will see." People come to Jesus on the testimony of others; Jesus enters their lives as a response to their deepest longing, and only after "staying" with him can they confess him as "Christ."

Praying with Scripture

- Samuel responds to God's call, "Speak, for your servant is listening." Pray for the grace to listen to the ways God continues to call you.

- Hear again in prayer the words of Jesus, "What are you looking for?"

- Pray over how your testimony may bring others to Christ.

Third Sunday in Ordinary Time

Readings: Jonah 3:1-5, 10; Ps 25:4-9; 1 Cor 7:29-31; Mark 1:14-20

> **"Guide me in your truth and teach me,**
> **for you are God my savior" (Ps. 25:5).**

A LIFE INTERRUPTED

Until Ash Wednesday the gospels of Cycle B follow Mark (1:14–3:6). Each of the four Gospels has distinctive literary characteristics, a particular picture of Jesus, and different understandings of discipleship. Mark, the shortest of the Gospels, contains the most vivid human portrayal of Jesus. He expresses deep emotions (which Matthew and Luke often omit): compassion, strong displeasure, surprise at disbelief, deep sighs, indignation, and ignorance of when history will end. Jesus is a powerful and mysterious presence whose actions constantly elicit wonder and surprise and evoke questions such as "Who is this?" (4:41). The narrative style harmonizes with the picture of Jesus—rapid scene changes with Jesus on the move, surrounded by crowds, announcing and enacting God's reign, narrated in short, staccato sentences with constant use of the connective "immediately."

But as the Gospel moves forward, the pace slows. After Jesus enters Jerusalem, time is measured in days; his final day is marked by hours, much like the brutal, antiseptic, execution watches so familiar at U.S. prisons. The figure, once powerful in word and deed, speaks only briefly, and his last words are, "My God, my God, why have you forsaken me?" The hands that once fed the hungry and restored life to a little girl are immobile, nailed to a cross.

Mark's introduction of Jesus (1:14-15) is a capsule summary of his whole Gospel. Jesus arrives after John had been arrested (literally "handed over"), a fate that will await Jesus himself and his followers after his death. He proclaims the "good news of [also from] God" (au. trans.), that is, a new privileged time *(kairos)*, when God's manifestation of power and care for the people (kingdom or reign) is at their

23

doorstep. He then summons them to a change of heart, to take a new look at their lives and put their trust in the good news. This is not simply a story from the past but a clarion call to readers.

This new beginning encompasses two prototypical events: the calling of the first disciples (1:16-20) and the confrontation with evil (1:21-28). The calling, heavily influenced by the compelling calls of prophets (Isa 6:1-13; Jer 1:14-19), is an icon of discipleship. Jesus is not a solitary prophet but one who calls companions; he enters the lives of four people engaged in their ordinary occupations, simply saying, "Follow me" (with a hint of their commission to "become fishers"), and they immediately drop everything to follow. Discipleship involves "being with" Jesus and doing the things of Jesus.

The call also inaugurates the story of the disciples, which, along with the story of Jesus, provides the great drama of Mark. Though following enthusiastically, their fate will be like that of the different hearers of the word in Mark 4:13-20. Satan will steal the commitment from some (8:33), some will fall away during persecution (14:27), and ultimately all will abandon Jesus at the cross. Mark is interested not only in portraying the power of Jesus to elicit an immediate response but wants to tell a story of the challenges and failures that can await people as they respond to this call.

PRAYING WITH SCRIPTURE

- How does Mark's Jesus most challenge you today? How would you respond to his call to "trust in the good news"?

- Envision how God has entered or might enter your life in such a way that you drop everything to embark on a new journey.

The Presentation of the Lord

Readings: Mal 3:1-4; Ps 24:7-10; Heb 2:14-18; Luke 2:22-40

**"Now, Master, you may let your servant go
in peace according to your word" (Luke 2:29).**

WHAT DOES THE FUTURE HOLD?

Celebrated forty days after Christmas, this feast has assumed many different meanings throughout history. Once called the "Purification" from Luke's description of the completion of the days for "their purification" and from the citation by Luke of Leviticus (12:2-8), it has also been called Candlemas. The stress now, however, is to view Jesus' presentation as a fulfillment of Malachi's prophecy of the coming to the Temple of "the Lord whom you seek."

The gospel narrates the Lukan conclusion to the infancy cycle of the coming of Jesus as fulfillment of the hopes and expectations of the people. These narratives begin with Zechariah in the Temple and end with Anna and Simeon there, symbolizing God's presence among *ʿanawim,* people of little earthly power and influence who rely on God.

The earlier description of the feast, the Purification, causes some disquiet today, as if there were something unclean about childbirth. Since the Torah calls people to worship the living and life-giving God, anything that implies or mimics death, such as flowing blood or deathly pallor (leprosy), is "unclean," that is, the opposite of the holiness of God. Since childbirth was a liminal situation between life and death, especially in a culture with frequent infant and maternal death, while at the same time the gift of new life, surviving children were consecrated to God. Rather than purification, the reading focuses on Mary as one who consecrates her child to God.

The drama of the story is provided by the presence and proclamation of the two elderly people Simeon and Anna, who symbolize a life of expectant fidelity. Simeon, not a priest or Temple official but simply a righteous and devout person, awaits God's consolation, living out of faith in a revelation that he would not die before seeing God's Messiah. Seeing Mary and Joseph come, he takes the child in his arms and blesses God, uttering what has become the beautiful prayer of the funeral liturgy, *Nunc Dimittis,* "Now, Lord, you may let your servant go in peace," but then turns to Mary and predicts that the consolation brought to Israel will be a source of division and suffering and that a sword will pierce her heart. When I read these lines, I think of every mother standing at a baptismal font, knowing that the joy and new life now experienced and expected will include times of sorrow and trial.

Also standing before a youthful Joseph and Mary is Anna, an eighty-four-year-old prophetess who had spent her whole life in the Temple. Though her words are not recorded, she gives thanks to God and speaks out to "all who were awaiting the redemption of Israel." This coupling of Simeon and Anna reflects the frequent Lukan technique of joining stories in which a man and a woman are central; for example, Mary prays a canticle as does Zechariah.

Like all the stories of Luke's infancy narrative, this one offers rich resources for prayer and actualization. Mary and Joseph are Jews faithful to the Law of their ancestors, reminding us again how rooted Christianity is in Judaism. Young parents and faithful old people are brought together by the presence of Jesus, a challenging image for us today. Young parents who present their children to God at baptism can reflect on and pray over the future that will unfold for this child with its joys and sorrows and ask for God's help when the sword will pierce their hearts. Simeon and Anna provide wonderful images of older people who treasure past promises but also live with eager expectation of how God can continue to enter their lives. Such hope produces the paradox of letting go and waiting.

I recall over a decade ago when my mother at eighty-nine was dying of a brain tumor. In the final weeks of her life, she uttered frequently a simple prayer: "My God is beautiful and I will see my God." The feast of the Presentation, with its rich tradition of lighted candles, reminds us of our own ultimate coming into the presence of a God of beauty and love.

PRAYING WITH SCRIPTURE

- Pray over ways that you may present yourself before God with your hopes for the future.

- Pray in gratitude for older people who have kept the promise alive in love and hope.

- As a young mother Mary was faced with the prospect of suffering (a piercing sword). Pray especially for young parents who are confronted by anguish and grief.

Fifth Sunday in Ordinary Time

Readings: Job 7:1-4, 6-7; Ps 147:1-6; 1 Cor 9:16-19, 22-23;
Mark 1:29-39.

> **"He heals the brokenhearted**
> **and binds up their wounds" (Ps 147:3).**

COMPASSIONATE IN WORD AND DEED

Very few topics occupy the American consciousness as much as health care and the onset of debilitating illness, a concern of the readings for this Sunday. The tone is set by Job's lament of endless suffering and sleepless nights. The Gospels portray a Jesus who enters the world of the sick and suffering with healing touches and healing words. Even though Mark is the shortest of the Gospels, it contains the highest proportion of miracle stories, told often in vivid detail, that alert the readers to the extraordinary power of God manifest in Jesus.

The gospel narrates in compact form the healing of Simon's mother-in-law. Jesus is told of her illness, and without speaking a word, he goes over to her, grasps her hand, and helps her up. The fever leaves, and immediately she begins to serve them (NAB, "waited on"). Given Mark's tendency to communicate deeper meanings, hidden from outsiders (4:10-12), Mark's readers may see the house as an anticipation of their evening gatherings in house churches, and the service of the woman as an anticipation of the diaconal service of women in the community. The narrative also reminds us that the healing power of Jesus can be a liberation leading to greater service of others.

The following verses provide a scenic conclusion to the opening day of Jesus' proclamation of God's reign. Crowds of sick and possessed people (who are often equated in that culture) mass at the door, and Jesus heals various diseases and casts out demons, enjoining silence upon them. He then leaves "very early before dawn" (the subsequent hour of his death sentence and of the discovery of the empty tomb

[15:1; 16:2]) and retreats to a deserted place, where he had earlier been tested but where he now communes with God in prayer. The disciples find him, and he responds with a renewed commitment to his mission of proclamation and confronting the power of evil.

PRAYING WITH SCRIPTURE

- Pray especially for someone you know who is suffering a serious, isolating illness, and ask how God may call you to touch his or her life.

- Amid suffering, pray like the lamenting Job with the realization that "complaining" to God is a deep form of faith.

Sixth Sunday in Ordinary Time

Readings: Lev 13:1-2, 44-46; Ps 32:1-2, 5, 11; 1 Cor 10:31–11:1;
Mark 1:40-45

"Be glad in the LORD and rejoice, you just" (Ps 32:11).

CROSSING BARRIERS IN LOVE

A new day begins with the healing of a leper. Leprosy was not the modern Hansen's disease but designated a large number of scaly skin diseases. Still, these caused terror, and the excerpts from Leviticus 13 describe the social stigma attached to lepers as "unclean," forcing them to live at the margin of society. For contemporary people, ancient Jewish purity laws are both confusing and often the source of anti-Semitism. Purity is not primarily a moral category but a religious one; it is synonymous often with holiness, which is not, as in our thought, simply a moral category but more a zone of power that evokes awe and mystery.

The opposite of purity is uncleanness, which is not always sin. The leper, for example, is unclean but not called a sinner. God is primarily the source of life and the all-holy One. What affronts God and creation is unclean. In early rabbinic texts corpse impurity is "the father of the father of all uncleanness" and an offense to the living God. Purity laws surround symbols and carriers of life, and the "leper's" impurity arises because of the debilitation and white skin pallor, an intimation of death. Since impurity could be contagious, leprosy was an especially tragic condition that isolated people from loved ones and society.

Despite his social isolation, the leper approaches Jesus, kneels and utters words of courage and faith: "If you wish, you can make me clean" (Mark 1:40). Jesus then reacts "with compassion." (This is a better translation than the NAB's "moved with pity.") Compassion is the ability to identify with a suffering person and to enter the person's world with care and love. This is reflected in Jesus' first action of stretching out his hand, bridging the gap between the holy and the unclean by actually touching the man. Only then does he pronounce the healing words. The leprosy leaves, but Jesus "warns him sternly" to keep silent and fulfill the Jewish prescriptions for verification of a cure. The Greek of "stern warning" can also mean "groaning with anger," which some commentators interpret as Jesus' anger at the social conventions surrounding the disease. The man's paradoxical violation of Jesus' command and public proclamation continues the theme that the power of God present in Jesus is both explosive and contagious.

These readings pose special challenges today, especially in a health-obsessed culture in which the ancient attribution of illness to sin is now modernized by attributing it to a faulty lifestyle. (The promise of immortality lies in daily exercise and large helpings of broccoli!). Also, today people approach Jesus in courage and prayer for healing like the leper but still remain sick. Yet these readings provide hope. The story of Job, a righteous sufferer, breaks the link between suffering and guilt and gives people permission to lament before their God.

A Jesus who enacts God's reign among the broken and marginal people of his time is an enduring challenge for the contemporary Church. Equally, a Jesus who acts with compassionate words and touch is critical today. Often people diagnosed with horrible illnesses such as AIDS or different forms of cancer experience a sense of isolation; friends and even family react with fear and caution. Yet Jesus stretches out his hand and touches someone suffering social and religious isolation. He restores Simon's mother-in-law to her family and allows the leper to live again with dignity in the human community. Contemporary miracles of healing are often a compassionate word or touch and the gift of continued presence and welcome to sufferers by the community of family and Church.

Praying with Scripture

- At times of fear and illness prayerfully remember the courageous leper who both cried out to God in his suffering, and proclaimed Christ.

- Pray in gratitude for someone whose courage and faith in illness has led you to appreciate more deeply the power of God's love.

God's love is constant.

Seventh Sunday in Ordinary Time

Readings: Isa 43:18-19, 21-22, 24b-25; Ps 41:2-5, 13-14;
2 Cor 1:18-22; Mark 2:1-12

"We have never seen anything like this" (Mark 2:12).

HOMECOMING FOR A FORGIVEN SINNER

Sin, forgiveness, faith, suffering, healing—these powerful themes resonate throughout the readings for this Sunday. In a condensed masterpiece of poetry and theology, Second Isaiah summons to faith in a God who does something new and unheard of, not only by delivering the people from exile but by acting as one who, though "burdened" and "wearied" with the sins and crimes of the people, announces, "It is I, I, who wipe out, / for my own sake your offenses; / your sins I remember no more" (Isa 43:25). This rhythm of human turning away from God and divine reaching out with compassion and forgiveness is pervasive in the Bible: "Though your sins be like scarlet, / they may become white as snow; / though they be crimson red, / they may become white as wool" (Isa 1:18).

Today's gospel presents one of the longest and most vivid stories of forgiveness in the Synoptics. Mark's miracle accounts should be read like parables summoning us to place ourselves in the scene, to identify with the characters (even the less attractive ones), and to ask how the story challenges our lives. The narrative begins with Jesus "at home" in the lakeside village of Capernaum, preaching the word in a packed home (considerably smaller than an average living room today). We are given a glimpse outside the house and see four men carrying a paralyzed person on a simple cloth mattress (NAB: "mat"). Jesus' "sermon" is dramatically interrupted as the thatched roof is torn apart and the disabled man is lowered at his feet. This highlights the Markan theme that the faith that draws suffering people to Jesus often overcomes barriers (cf. 5:25-28; 10:48).

Mark writes that when Jesus saw this faith he said to the young man, "Child your sins are sent away" (NAB: "forgiven"). The focus of the story then shifts from a miracle of healing, which resumes in verse 11, to a controversy over the power to pronounce the forgiveness of sin. Though this may reflect conflicts between Mark's community and Judaism some forty years after the death of Jesus, Mark uses it to teach deeper meanings of forgiveness.

Forgiveness is a divine prerogative, as the scribes correctly note when they accuse Jesus of blasphemy. Mark stresses the power of Jesus, who knows the inner thoughts of the scribes and challenges them by pointing to the divine power to restore health as a sign of forgiveness. He turns again to the paralytic with three resounding commands: "Rise," "Take up your stretcher," and "Go home." This causes the crowds to glorify God. By weaving together a controversy over forgiveness with a healing narrative, Mark suggests that God's reign, now enacted in Jesus, brings a forgiveness that is granted in ways that can shock religious traditions.

On the narrative level, this story summons us initially to identify with the plight of the paralyzed man. The late novelist and essayist Andre Dubus, who was crippled in an auto accident, describes the pain of paralysis: "When you are carried, your helplessness and the very meatness of you slap your soul. And it is a frightening surrender to other arms and legs" (*Meditations from a Movable Chair* [Alfred A. Knopf, 1998]). Dependent on the care of others, Mark's paralytic is lifted to the roof and lowered precariously before Jesus, who praises the faith of the litter-bearers. The symbolism is rich here. The journey toward spiritual and physical healing often begins by support from the faith of others and involves the courage to let go and be carried by them. While paralysis is not a divine punishment, sin can be a form of paralysis, an inability to move. The experience of forgiveness, on the other hand, enables a person to rise up and return home with dignity. Sin is isolation and alienation, forgiveness is homecoming.

Mark offers an even deeper reflection on forgiveness. He tells his readers that Jesus is the Son of Man, who has authority on earth to forgive sin and is described as a blasphemer. "Son of Man" on earth describes the human Jesus who gives his very life as a ransom that others may be free (Mark 10:45). This first major conflict with the religious authorities foreshadows that moment when Jesus will be condemned as a blasphemer (14:64). Mark stresses that the cost of forgiveness offered by Jesus was his life blood poured out on the cross. When we gather for our weekly celebration of the paschal mystery, often paralyzed in different ways and needing to be borne up by the faith of others, we are summoned to hear again those words of Jesus, "Child, your sins are forgiven"; "Rise up"; "Walk."

PRAYING WITH SCRIPTURE

- Ponder Jesus' words to the paralytic and recall moments of experienced forgiveness that freed you to rise up and walk.

- Remember how you have been carried by the faith of others or have helped to carry others in their suffering.

- Explore how we are often like the scribes by questioning in our hearts the extent of God's forgiving love.

Eighth Sunday in Ordinary Time

Readings: Hos 2:16b, 17b, 21-22; Ps 103:1-4, 8, 10, 12-13;
2 Cor 3:1b-6; Mark 2:18-22

"I will lead her into the desert / and speak to her heart"
(Hos 2:16).

A WEDDING INVITATION: PLEASE RESPOND!

With Lent around the corner, it is not a time when we think of weddings, yet nuptial imagery sets the tone for the liturgy. In the first reading the eighth-century prophet Hosea enacts in his life God's enduring
love for a people that has turned away to worship Canaanite gods (Hebrew: baals, "masters"). God commands Hosea, "Go, take a harlot
wife / . . . for the land gives itself to harlotry, / turning away from the
LORD" (1:2). It is debated whether this is a command to marry a prosti-
tute, to seek out an unfaithful wife, or is purely a prophetic allegorical
vision.

Whatever the interpretation, the focus of the narrative is God's desire to "allure her; / I will and lead her [Israel] into the desert / and
speak to her heart" (2:16) in order to renew the marriage covenant of
love with her. The people will now call God, "My husband," not "My
master" (Hebrew: *baal;* 2:18). God will renew the people in right and in
justice (a couplet that suggests right relation to God and concern for the
vulnerable in the community), in love ("steadfast love," a prime covenant quality), in mercy (tender mercy or compassion, the feeling that a
woman has for the child of her womb), and fidelity or enduring care.
These divine qualities, repeated in the responsorial psalm, offer the
most condensed and eloquent biblical descriptions of God and, as
covenant promises, are to shape the lives of individuals and communities.

The gospel offers a collection of sayings in which Jesus defends his
actions against objections of the scribes and Pharisees. Such material

reflects two different periods: the first, during Jesus' lifetime, when there were disputes between Jesus and particular Jewish groups; the second, an era of growing estrangement between Judaism and Christianity some forty years later, when the Gospels were being composed.

Fasting is associated with rites of mourning, repentance, or prayers of supplication and symbolizes self-effacement and trust in God. Fasting expresses also a longing for the final or eschatological intervention of God in history. The image of Jesus as bridegroom picks up the Old Testament motif of God's spousal love for the people of Israel and also anticipates the messianic age, which in Jewish writings contemporary with Jesus is symbolized by a wedding banquet. Jesus' response affirms that his presence in history is the beginning of this final age (Mark 1:14-15), a wedding time of feasting, not fasting, and of rejoicing, when ordinary life is suspended. In parabolic that show Jesus as a keen observer of ordinary human life, he compares this new situation to repairing old (most likely leather) garments with a new patch that will rip off as the leather ages or with putting fermenting wine into worn-out skins that will then burst.

Mark's readers, like ourselves, exist at a time when the bridegroom has been taken away and the new messianic age has not arrived in its fullness. It was also a time of that growing estrangement between Judaism and nascent Christianity whose effects the Church is only now confronting, since Christian anti-Semitism has sadly been fostered by Paul's reference to the "letter that brings death," which the following verses identify with the Mosaic covenant. In the Vatican document "We Remember: A Reflection on the Shoah" (1998), the Church recognizes the tradition of anti-Semitism, saying that "despite the Christian preaching of love for all, the prevailing mentality for centuries punished minorities." In announcing the Great Jubilee, Pope John Paul II called for a time of rejoicing but also for repentance over the acquiescence by the Church "to intolerance and even the use of violence in the service of truth" (*Tertio Millenio Adveniente*, no. 35).

The deeper meaning of repentance and the path to mutual love and respect between Jew and Christian emerge from Hosea and Psalm 103. When we are unfaithful, a loving God seeks us out in the wilderness and speaks to our hearts, offering a renewed relationship in justice, steadfast love, tender mercy, and enduring fidelity. This is the God of Israel and the Father of Jesus, the Christ, the bridegroom who has not simply been taken away but "loved the church and handed himself over for her" (Eph 5:25). The God who renews the Church through searching love is the new wine that shatters the contemporary wineskins of shrunken visions.

PRAYING WITH SCRIPTURE

- Pray quietly over the word "God." Notice if the images that come to mind are those of Hosea and the psalm. Repeat quietly and prayerfully these images. Let God speak to your heart.

- As the Lenten season approaches, think of ways in which we have deadened the command of love and acquiesced to intolerance and even violence.

- Bring forth in prayer your deepest hopes for new wine and fresh wineskins.

Ash Wednesday

Readings: Joel 2:12-18; Ps 51:3-6, 12-14, 17; 2 Cor 5:20–6:2;
Matt 6:1-6, 16-18

"Rend your hearts . . . and return" (Joel 2:13).

RISING FROM THE ASHES!

Ash Wednesday inaugurates not simply the forty days preceding
Easter but the whole ninety-day paschal cycle, which extends beyond
Easter seven weeks until Pentecost. The Lectionary cycle grew backward and forward from the central celebration of Easter. There is one
mystery—the death of Jesus, his resurrection, and the gift of the Spirit.
One of the major contributions of the Second Vatican Council was the
recovery of Lent and Eastertide as one extended celebration of Christian initiation into and rededication to the paschal mystery.

The theme for Ash Wednesday is sounded by the call to public repentance in Joel, ". . . return to me with your whole heart . . . / rend
your hearts, not your garments" (Joel 2:12-13). Ordinary life is to cease,
symbolized by the fast and the assembly of all people, including
newlyweds and infants. The gospel speaks of prayer and almsgiving,
which, together with fasting, make up the traditional triad of Lenten
observances. Fasting and almsgiving touch on two fundamental drives
of human life for nourishment and ownership. Sacrificing them involves an act of trust in God that is sustained only by prayer.

This day has become a virtual sacrament of Catholic identity, as people
throng churches to "get ashes," which, paradoxically, is just what the
gospel counsels against—external signs of devotion.

Still, Karl Rahner has captured eloquently the meaning of this sign:
"When on Ash Wednesday we hear the words, 'Remember, you are
dust,' we are also told that we are brothers and sisters of the incarnate
Lord. In these words we are told everything that we are: nothingness
that is filled with eternity; death that teems with life; futility that re-
deems; dust that is God's life forever" (*The Eternal Year*, p. 62).

PRAYING WITH SCRIPTURE

- Discuss/pray together as a family or a community about how the traditional practices of Lent may take on new life: setting aside part of a food budget for groups concerned with hunger; "giving up" that most precious commodity, "busy time," to be present to others.

- Pick one of the seven "penitential psalms" (Psalms 6, 32, 38, 51, 102, 130, 143) and pray it, thinking not only of personal sinfulness but of the sins that mar our world.

First Sunday of Lent

Readings: Gen 9:8-15; Ps 25:4-9; 1 Pet 3:18-22; Mark 1:12-15

> **"Your ways, O LORD, make known to me;
> teach me your paths" (Ps 25:4).**

A JOURNEY BEGINS!

From Lent to Pentecost the readings are determined by the seasonal feasts. In all cycles the first two Sundays present the temptation and transfiguration of Jesus, which form a virtual epitome of the Christology of the season. Jesus, taking on human form, humbled himself even to death and was "tested" by his Father, yet this was a presage of his glorification. From the third to the fifth Sundays, two options are available. Churches with catechumens preparing for baptism can choose the great "coming to faith" stories of the Samaritan woman (John 4), the man born blind (John 9) and the raising of Lazarus (John 11) from Cycle A, or follow those chosen for year B or C. In year B, the final three Sundays, all from the Gospel of John, focus more intensely on the paschal mystery. The Old Testament readings present four cardinal figures and events of saving history (covenants with Noah, Moses at Sinai, and Jeremiah's promise of the new covenant, the testing and blessing of Abraham). Compressed in the Lenten readings are themes, motifs and figures that resound throughout Scripture. The Lenten pilgrimage is best made with the Bible as a guide book.

Today's Old Testament reading concludes the long story of the great flood (Gen 6:9–9:29) when all living creatures, apart from those saved by Noah, are destroyed. It occurs within the primeval history (Genesis 1–11), which tells how God created the world and a community of men and women with a destiny to care for the earth and to experience divine intimacy. Tragically humanity turns away from God, inaugurating a rhythm of human sin and self-destructiveness, which is countered by renewed blessing from God. But out of the waters of destruction a new beginning emerges when God makes a covenant with "you and your descendants after you and with every living creature that was with you: all the birds, and the various tame and wild animals that were with you and came out of the ark . . . that never again shall all bodily creatures be destroyed by the waters of a flood."

This Noachian covenant is a universal promise to all living creatures prior to their division by race, religion, and language (Gen 11:1-9). The covenant and rescue through water foreshadow baptism (1 Pet 3:20-21). By embracing all non-human life, the covenant is a mandate calling for deep respect toward all people and care for our earth. God promises that the world will not be destroyed by water; there is no assurance that human misuse will not bring this about. This covenant is also the foundation of the particular covenants that will unfold and captures the marriage of universalism and particularism in biblical revelation: Abraham will be the father of many nations; Israel after Sinai is to be a light to the nations; Jesus will enact a new covenant that will benefit the whole of humanity.

Mark's brief narrative of the temptation of Jesus, followed by his opening proclamation, is a condensed anticipation of major themes of his Gospel. The traditional term "temptation" is inaccurate, since the original Greek means "tested" or "subjected to a trial." This evokes the wider theme of God's testing of the people of Israel (also like Jesus in the desert), the servant of Isaiah 53, and the suffering just person, who though tested by God remains faithful and is called a child of God (Wis 2:12-20; 5:1-23). In this first Lenten gospel the Church portrays a Jesus who "because he himself was tested through what he suffered . . . is able to help those who are being tested" (Heb 2:18).

Jesus leaves the desert to proclaim the "good news," a term used in secular Greek for the public proclamation of a major event (for example, the visit of an emperor) and in Second Isaiah to proclaim the liberating love of God for the returning exiles (Isa 52:7; 61:1). The news is good because God's "reigning" is at hand. This recalls the image of God as king who protects an endangered people, has special concern for the vulnerable, and judges violence and injustice (Pss 72 and 95–100). Mark does not tell us just what God's reign involves. Only by following the way of Jesus through the Gospel, hearing his word, and adopting his values can a person understand more deeply the mystery of God's reign (Mark 4:10). The beginning of this journey through the Gospel and through Lent calls for *metanoia*—repentance or a second look at life—and belief, an act of trust in the God who guides the unfolding journey.

PRAYING WITH SCRIPTURE

- Once the favorite Catholic question was, What have you "given up" for Lent? Now we might ask, Can we "give in" to the ways God may be trying to touch our lives?

- At moments of trial and testing, place yourself in the desert alone with Jesus, our compassionate high priest, who is able "to sympathize with our weakness" because he "has similarly been tested in every way" (Heb 4:15).

- Pray over ways in which we as a nation may renew the covenant of care and respect with all living beings.

Second Sunday of Lent

Readings: Gen 22:1-2, 9a, 10-13, 15-18; Ps 116:10, 15-19;
Rom 8:31b-34; Mark 9:2-10

"If God is for us, who can be against us?" (Rom 8:31).

AFTER VISION, A JOURNEY CONTINUES

The readings present a compendium of themes that shape the Lenten season. The first reading concludes the cycle of narratives about Abraham (Gen 12–23), which unfold from his call, with the promise that he and Sarah will be the parents of many nations, through the covenant and the birth of a son, the bearer of the promise (Isaac), and reaches its pinnacle in God's command that Abraham offer Isaac as a holocaust. As one of the most treasured subjects of Christian art, the denouement of the story is familiar. At the last moment "the Lord's messenger" intervenes; Isaac is spared, and the promise is renewed: "Because you acted as you did in not withholding from me your beloved son, I will bless you abundantly" (Gen 22:16-17).

In both Judaism and Christianity Abraham is a paradigm of faith who "when tested was found loyal" (Sir 44:20), who "hoped against hope" (Rom 4:18), and who "by faith, . . . when put to the test, offered up Isaac" because he believed in a God who could raise up the dead (Heb 11:17-19). Also in Jewish tradition Isaac is transformed into a model of self-sacrifice who went willingly to his death, which is adopted by Christians for Jesus, "the Son of God" who "has loved me and given himself up for me" (Gal 2:20).

"Transformation" would be a better term to describe today's gospel story, since Jesus, though in the form of God, took on the "form" of a slave (Phil 2:6-7), and is now transformed and seen as an exalted member of the heavenly court. The narrative is dense with biblical allusions. The dazzling white clothes are a symbol of divine presence in Daniel 7:9, while the presence of Elijah and Moses has been interpreted in a

43

number of ways. They are symbols of the prophets and the Law; both are people who did not taste death but were exalted to heaven (Elijah in 2 Kings 2:1-12; Moses in extra-biblical tradition); they are faithful prophets who suffered because they followed God's word.

The deeper focus of the account emerges from the divine voice: "This is my beloved Son. Listen to him" (Mark 9:7). The transformation follows the first of three predictions by Jesus of his death by crucifixion, which the disciples consistently resist. Peter's desire for three booths seems an attempt to substitute divine presence for the way of the cross. The same three disciples who witness Jesus' transformation fail to watch with him during his agony in the garden (Mark 14:32-42). Mark's readers and we ourselves are to hear the voice of a Jesus who says that the way to glory is only through the cross.

The narrative is also followed by one of the most dramatic stories in the Gospel (Mark 9:14-29), the exorcism from a young boy of a destructive demon which the disciples of Jesus are powerless to combat. Raphael's magnificent panorama "The Transfiguration," which greets visitors to the Vatican museums, captures the sequence perfectly. While Jesus and the heavenly companions are illumined in resplendent colors, the fruitless struggle of the disciples with the demon occupy the lower right-hand corner. The eye cannot help but behold the chaos of earthly evil when looking at heavenly glory.

The Transfiguration is not, as some homilists state, a kind of midpoint encouragement to the disciples, since they will continue to misunderstand Jesus and will flee at his arrest; and Peter denies him. The deeper meaning of the narrative for Mark and for us during Lent is that even after moments of transcendence and transformation, we must come back to earth, continue to hear the voice of Jesus, and follow him on the way to the cross. Experience of transcendence is juxtaposed with the struggle against evil.

The readings today encourage deep faith and trust in God. Poignant and powerful is the faith of an aging Abraham, ordered by the same God who promised multiple progeny to kill the son who was to continue the promise. And yet such a mystery of total self-giving is rooted in the very nature of God, "who did not spare his own Son but handed him over *for us*." The final transformation in Mark is not another heavenly vision but a youth clothed in white announcing from a tomb: "You seek Jesus of Nazareth, the crucified. He has been raised; he is not here" (16:6). At the very door of death, a message of life is proclaimed. Believing this is the ultimate challenge of Lent.

PRAYING WITH SCRIPTURE

- Recall in prayer moments of transformation when a sense of the beauty and transcendence of God touched your life, followed perhaps by down-to-earth experiences that remain a challenge to faith.

- Pray with the Lenten motifs of these readings:

  — Abraham, a model of a lifelong journey of faith that was tested to the very end;

  — the disciples who, though intimate with Jesus, crumbled when faced with the mystery of the cross;

  — the mystery of a God who demands ultimate self-surrender but who gave an only-begotten Son up to the horror of rejection and death.

Third Sunday of Lent

Readings: Exod 20:1-17 or Exod 20:1-3, 7-8, 12-17; Ps 19:8-11;
1 Cor 1:22-25; John 2:13-25

"The law of the LORD is perfect, / refreshing the soul"
(Ps 19:8).

WHAT IS TRUE RELIGION?

Over twenty years ago I was giving a series of Scripture workshops in South Africa during the worst period of apartheid (shortly after the murder of Steve Biko). Yet the hope and joy of an oppressed people shone forth in every liturgy and during every occasion when we shared insights on Scripture. On my last day, after Sunday Mass in Johannesburg, I struck up a conversation with a lively young couple who had just returned from the United States. After initial pleasantries, they asked me what I honestly thought of South Africa. I mentioned the natural beauty and the vigor of all the people, but finally said that I was appalled by the racism and enforced living conditions of the African peoples. They then became a bit defensive and mentioned, accurately, that in the United States "black people" had harsh living conditions and were also doing mainly menial work. I simply said, "We don't have better hearts, but we do have better laws."

The readings today remind us initially of the importance of law to bring about respect for God and neighbor, and likewise warn us about the dangers that arise when commercial concerns are intertwined with religious devotion. The book of Exodus lists the Ten Commandments near the solemn conclusion of the Sinai covenant. Observing these commands is a response to the liberating love of God, "who brought you out of the land of Egypt, that place of slavery" (Exod 20:1). They unfold in two panels, one concerned with wholehearted love of God and rejection of idolatry, the other with relations of justice and care between neighbors. Even today these provide a foundation for human dignity and human rights, especially since Jesus redefines the neighbor as the stranger in need (Luke 10:25-37).

Today's gospel is one of the few narratives about Jesus that appear in all four Gospels, though in John it is placed at the beginning rather than at the end of Jesus' ministry. Even skeptical scholars admit that it has a historical foundation, but they debate its significance. Was it a symbolic prediction of the Temple's destruction, a prophetic attack cleansing the Temple from mercantile misuse or an abortive attempt at an armed takeover of the Temple? The Johannine account, in which Jesus quotes Zechariah 14:21, "stop making my Father's house a market-place" (John 2:16), seems at first glance to support the interpretation of the event as a cleansing. Other Jewish groups at the time of Jesus also criticized abuses by the Temple establishment. Yet, as so often in John, the issue quickly becomes not what Jesus did but *who he is*. "The Jews" ask what sign (authentication) can he give for doing this, and Jesus challenges them to destroy the Temple, and he will rebuild it in three days. Following the usual Johannine technique of misunderstanding, the narrator notes that Jesus was speaking of the temple of his body, which the disciples understood only after the resurrection.

The gospel contains other challenges. Since two Sunday gospel readings and the daily readings from now on in Lent come from John and focus on the growing opposition between Jesus and "the Jews," the anti-Semitic potential of the readings heightens. The expression "the Jews" in John stand primarily for Jewish leaders of the author's time, during the split between the emerging Christian Church and the synagogue near the end of the first century. The center of the dispute is the proclamation of the divinity of Jesus, which is a hallmark of John's theology. Since theological dispute rarely makes for charitable tolerance, the Jews and aspects of Judaism are literally demonized in John (8:44, "You are of your father the devil"). Today, after the horrors of the Holocaust and following the constant teaching of Pope John Paul II, preachers and teachers have an obligation to explain the historical setting of John's statements and to counter misuse of the Bible to foment hatred between peoples.

The three readings have been selected with a view to the Lenten schooling of catechumens preparing for baptism: the fundamental demands of Christian life embodied in the Decalogue, the "preaching of Christ crucified" (cf. 2 Cor 1:22), and the hope of resurrection. But they have enduring value for all members of the pilgrim Church. In a culture of autonomy and personal fulfillment, it is crucial that the deepest social values we share be translated into law. At times this can involve a form of "crucifixion," as people struggle against such evils as racism and the various assaults on life. The gospel also reminds us of the cost of prophetic criticism of the abuse of religious instutions. The late Raymond E. Brown, S.S., observed that if Jesus were to reappear with similar challenges today, those most likely to reject him would identify themselves as Christians and think of Jesus as an impostor (*The Death of the Messiah* [Doubleday, 1994] p. 393). Lent is a time not only to rejoice but also to repent of those evils that can lie close to the very heart of religious devotion.

Praying with Scripture

- As the midpoint of Lent draws near, reflect prayerfully on the biblical Decalogue in preparation for the sacrament of reconciliation.

- Pray quietly about Paul's message to the Corinthians, asking God to grant deep faith that the cross, "God's folly," is "wiser than men, and his weakness more powerful than men."

- What special challenges do the life and teaching of Jesus present to the religious practice of the Church today?

Fourth Sunday of Lent

Readings: 2 Chr 36:14-16, 19-23; Ps 137:1-6; Eph 2:4-10;
John 3:14-21

"By grace you have been saved through faith"
(Eph 2:8).

GRACE ABOUNDING

As Holy Week nears, the central theme of the liturgy today is captured by the second reading: "God, who is rich in mercy, because of the great love he had for us . . . brought us to life with Christ" (Eph 2:4-5). The first reading is the conclusion of the Chronicler's history, written around 400 B.C., almost two hundred years after the Babylonian Exile. It presents in capsule form the "sin history" which led to exile, an experience poignantly remembered in the responsorial psalm. Yet God's final word is not indictment of sin but the gift of liberation and return to the land of promise.

The central assertion of the gospel, "God so loved the world that he gave his only Son, so that everyone who believes in him might not perish but might have eternal life" (John 3:16), is one of the most cited New Testament texts, paraded at sporting events and on bumper stickers. It concludes a staged and dramatic dialogue between Nicodemus and Jesus. Nicodemus comes at night and praises Jesus, but Jesus says that no one can see the kingdom of God without being born from above *anōthen*. Since this Greek term can also mean "again," Nicodemus is described—using the familiar Johannine technique of misunderstanding that leads to deeper insight—as taking this to mean natural birth, to which Jesus responds that he is talking about being born of water and the Spirit. This is most likely an allusion to baptism. The frequent invocation of "born again" to refer to an adult renewal of faith and conversion by an already baptized Christian has no foundation in John. John is speaking of first baptism, which Jesus understands as "from above," that is, from God's gratuitous act of love.

Jesus' statement then leads into the enigmatic comparison of the lifting up (crucifixion) of the Son of Man to Moses' mounting of the serpent on a pole (Num 21:9) after the people were bitten by serpents as punishment for their rebellion against Moses. The comparison in John is *not* between Jesus and the serpent, but between the saving effect of the lifting up in both cases. The section from today's gospel then expands on the gift of eternal life that flows from belief in the exalted Son of Man.

In announcing God's love for the world, John's vision embraces the whole cosmos, not simply an elect people, so that "everyone" who believes may be saved. God's love is more dominant in the Johannine writings than anywhere else in the New Testament. God is love (1 John 4:8); love is the mutual relationship between Jesus and the Father (John 15:9-10; 17:23); Jesus loves his disciples and says that their love of service and friendship is to be a hallmark of discipleship (John 13:34-35; 15:12-14). The paschal season is the public affirmation and renewal of such love.

The concluding verses present the shadow side of Johannine theology: Whoever does not believe in Jesus has already been condemned, because they loved darkness more than light. They embody John's "realized eschatology" in which judgment occurs during the ministry of Jesus rather than at the end of history (cf. Matt 25:31-46, "sheep and goats"). They also reflect controversies in John's community over explicit belief in the divinity of Jesus. When interpreted in a fundamentalist sense, these comments lead to a sectarian theology of salvation and an incorrect understanding of mission and evangelization.

The readings provide ample material for preaching and reflection as Lent draws to a close. Simply put, they embody Paul's statement, "Where sin increased, grace overflowed all the more" (Rom 5:20). As a time of reconciliation, Lent and Easter remind us that no human evil is beyond the pale of God's love and that forgiveness is a gift; as a time of renewal, that we are God's handiwork created in Christ Jesus for . . . good works."

Praying with Scripture

- Hold a crucifix, the symbol of Christ's lifting up, and read prayerfully Ephesians 2:4-10.

- Pray for the grace to experience more deeply that overwhelming sense of forgiving love that is more powerful than any sin.

- In your Lenten journey, recall and walk again with those who touched your life and now experience a loving God, who welcomed them to "eternal life."

Fifth Sunday of Lent

Readings: Jer 31:31-34; Ps 51:3-4, 12-15; Heb 5:7-9; John 12:20-33

**"Give me back the joy of your salvation,
and a willing spirit sustain in me" (Ps 51:14).**

WHAT WOULD JESUS DO?

In these last two weeks of Lent, the readings draw our eyes to the crucified one, with a focus on what God has done for us. The promise of the new covenant embodies the aging Jeremiah's spiritual testament to an exiled people: that even though they have sinned in the past, "I will be their God, and they shall be my people" (Jer 31:33). It will be written on the hearts of the people, and their acceptance will not be taught but will arise from their deep experience of forgiveness, "for I will forgive their evildoing and remember their sin no more." Though the term "new covenant" appears only here in the Old Testament, at the Last Supper Jesus will describe his self-offering as a new covenant (Luke 22:20; 1 Cor 11:25).

Today's gospel concludes John's presentation of the public ministry of Jesus and provides the bridge to the story of his final days. The Greeks who would like to "see" Jesus underscore the universal dimension of the lifting up and glorification of the Son of Man, when "I will draw everyone to myself." Having witnessed both the sadness of death and triumph over it (described in the preceding story of Lazarus) and having reached the hour of his imminent death, Jesus now speaks of the paradox of life through death. As the springtime festival of Passover nears, Jesus points to the mystery of the grain of wheat, which, after seeming to lie dead in the soil, now springs up throughout the land to sustain life. This dying and rising provides a paradigm for discipleship. Whoever loves his life will lose it, and whoever hates it will gain eternal life. These words seem jarring to an age aware of the dangers of self-loathing and lack of self-esteem. "Loving life" in John does not refer to the proper sense of dignity and joy that one should have as a graced person; it means a preference for "the world" and human glory that can blind a person to God's love. Hatred of one's life means rejection of the claims of the "world" and willingness to serve and follow Jesus. This becomes explicit in the next saying, "whoever serves me, must follow me."

This cost of losing one's life touches Jesus himself as he speaks, in the Synoptic Gospels' accounts of the events in Gethsemane, from the depths of his troubled soul, "Father, save me from this hour," while accepting that it was for the glory of his Father that he has come to the hour of his passion. As at his baptism in Mark, the barrier between heaven and earth is bridged, and a heavenly voice accepts Jesus' offering, which Jesus then says was "for your sake," since by his death the power of evil will be broken.

The reading from the letter to the Hebrews plays a similar symphony about the passion in a different key. It speaks of Jesus "in the days when [he] was in the flesh," a biblical expression for the sphere of weakness and suffering to which Christ was subject as he prayed to the One who could save him from death. This does not mean avoiding physical death but rescue from the power and realm of death. In Hebrews Jesus is a compassionate high priest who shares flesh and blood with God's sons and daughters, and who was himself tested through what he suffered so that he could help others equally tested (Heb 2:14-16). Today's reading says that Jesus "learned obedience" from what he suffered. Biblical obedience is not primarily following the will of another but a "deep listening"—in the case of Jesus, not only to his Father but, as the compassionate one, to the sufferings of his brothers and sisters. His life and suffering were a school of deep listening and compassion. This is the Jesus whose loving service and enduring presence we celebrate over the next two weeks.

The readings lead us into the deepest mysteries of Christian faith: the allure of "the world," the inevitability of death and suffering, even the call to embrace it, along with the ringing paradox that loss of human life is the gain of eternal life; that we have a compassionate high priest, whose soul was also troubled as he faced the abyss of death but whose death was an enduring covenant of forgiveness inscribed with the promise that "where I am, there also will my servant be" (John 12:26).

PRAYING WITH SCRIPTURE

- In the world around him Jesus saw signs of new life arising from death. Pray about such signs in our world today.

- Jesus, the compassionate one, learned "deep listening" from his suffering. Recall moments when suffering became a school of compassion for you.

- Read prayerfully Psalm 51, asking the God of mercy and love to create a clean heart and a willing spirit.

Palm Sunday of the Lord's Passion

Readings: Isa 50:4-7; Ps 22:8-9, 17-20, 23-24; Phil 2:6-11;
Mark 14:1–15:47 [or 15:1-39]; BLESSINGS OF PALMS: *Mark 11:1-10*
or *John 12:12-16*

"He emptied himself,
taking the form of a slave" (Phil 2:7).

WALKING THE WALK

The cumbersome title given to this day in the latest revision of the
Lectionary, Palm Sunday of the Lord's Passion, captures the dual aspect of the liturgical celebration. The processional rite of blessing and
carrying palms describes Jesus' triumphal entry into Jerusalem in what
will be the last week of his earthly life, which then unfolds in the reading of the Passion.

The liturgy is dense with symbolism and fraught with paradox. Wav-
ing of palms evokes memories of the feast of Tabernacles, when people
waved branches and sang the Hallel (Psalms 113–118) to commemorate
liberation from Egypt or of the victorious entry of the Maccabees into
Jerusalem to rededicate the Temple (1 Macc 13:51; 2 Macc 10:7). Yet the
crowds that call to Jesus, "Hosanna," ("Save us, we pray") will cry
loudly for his death in barely five days. The image of a royal messiah
who is not a warlike figure but a bearer of peace seated on "an ass's
colt" inaugurates a week when Jesus will die between two "revolution-
aries."

Another paradox is that the Passion narratives that stand at the foun-
tainhead of the Gospel tradition and are rich in theological insight and
narrative power are proclaimed only twice each year. Each narrative
has its distinctive characteristics. Mark narrates vividly Jesus' anguish
in the garden and does not flinch from the most brutal aspects of the
execution ritual (scourging, mocking, crowning with thorns). Yet he
writes from the viewpoint of Easter faith, which is rooted in the mystery

of the Cross. The Cross is salvation; the humiliation of Jesus is his exaltation (see Phil 2:6-11); the way of discipleship is the way of suffering, and while the called disciples flee, women who had followed him in Galilee stand at the cross; the proper confession of Jesus as Son of God is uttered by the Gentile centurion (15:39). Jesus dies with a cry, "My God, my God, why have you abandoned me?" (Ps 22:2), leaving readers to wonder whether this is truly despair or an unfinished lament that ends in triumphant hope (Ps 22:23-32).

John's Passion narrative (read on Good Friday) softens the harsh aspects of Jesus' sufferings by reducing the scourging and mocking to two verses (John 19:2-3). It is less a story of degradation than of the triumphal return of the Word to the Father and the hour of his glorification. Authority and majesty characterize Jesus as his captors fall before him. His death is the willing acceptance of the cup his Father has given him (18:11) and a triumphal victory over the powers of the world, as he interrogates his accusers, reducing them to the role of powerless questioners (18:38; 19:9-11). Jesus' death is a model of a friend who lays down his life for others (15:12-13), and his final words, "It is finished," are a sign that he has completed the work his Father gave him (5:36).

Though it is a week rich with biblical readings, Holy Week is also a time when diverse communities express the deepest mysteries of their faith by bodily movement—Palm Sunday processions, Stations of the Cross, the kissing of the cross, and dramatic reenactments of Jesus' journey to death, which often wind through city streets, especially in Hispanic communities such as the San Fernando Cathedral in San Antonio. There is the beautiful ceremony of Pésame (literally "weights or burdens"), in which parish groups join with Mary in prayer and song in bearing the burden of Jesus' death. A statue of Mary is dressed in black mourning clothes, often made by someone in the parish who has lost a son or loved one, while people are invited to share grief and offer words of mutual consolation. In rhythmic song and movement African-American parishes ask, "Were you there when they crucified my Lord?" The Passion of Jesus moves beyond words and takes hold of the feet and hands, the lips and hearts of individuals and communities.

This week is a time to listen deeply to the readings, to pray over them, to let them become part of our lives as we confront the mystery of suffering. In a memorable paean to Christ's presence, Gerard Manley Hopkins wrote, "for Christ plays in ten thousand places,/ Lovely in limbs, and lovely in eyes not his/ To the Father through the features of men's faces." Holy Week reminds us that Christ also suffers in ten thousand places, broken in limbs and weeping in eyes not his.

PRAYING WITH SCRIPTURE

- Create in prayer a "way of the cross," perhaps from your own life, from the life of a loved one, or from the world around us. Visualize Christ's presence as you walk this way.

- Pray all of Psalm 22, entering deeply into the feelings of abandonment so that the deeper hope of God's help may emerge.

Easter Sunday

Readings: Acts 10:34a, 37-43; Ps 118:1-2, 16-17, 22-23; Col 3:1-4
or 1 Cor 5:6b-8; John 20:1-9 or Mark 16:1-7

**"This is the day the Lord has made;
let us rejoice and be glad" (Ps 118:1).**

It Doesn't Fit In!

While laboring through graduate studies, I lived at an extraordinary parish in Chicago, St. Thomas the Apostle, whose self-designation was "God's People in Wonderful Variety." The parish had exuberant and prayerful liturgies, especially during Holy Week and Easter. One Easter the children's liturgy featured different classes presenting their gifts to the risen Jesus. A class of fourth graders lumbered up the aisle with a stuffed teddy bear twice the size of the gift bearers. The bear then reclined serenely against the altar, facing the congregation. After the liturgy an irate parishioner phoned, appalled at the liturgy and especially the smiling teddy bear, and kept repeating, "It was a total surprise" that "simply did not fit in." After a few forays on my part into the themes of God's love for all creation and gratitude over the enthusiasm of children, the teddy bear remained insurmountable. Finally, with some resignation, I said, "You are absolutely right, it was a total surprise and simply did not fit in; but neither does resurrection from the dead."

The selections from the Acts of the Apostles and Paul proclaim the profound meanings of the resurrection: God has raised up Jesus; we have been raised up "in company with Christ." The ancient horror of death has been overcome; God's gift of life can never be snatched away. The gospels (from John and Mark) proclaim the same message as narrative theology.

Mark proclaims this most simply with the paschal proclamation: "You seek Jesus of Nazareth, the crucified. He has been raised; he is not here" (Mark 16:6). The place of death cannot contain Jesus. In ancient thought a tomb is not simply a place where a body is put; it is the entrance to the realm of the dead. The empty tomb is a vivid symbol that this realm has been emptied of its power.

John's Gospel greets us in the waning darkness of the night as morning approaches. Mary Magdalene, who is the first to the tomb in every Gospel account, notices that the tomb is empty and announces to Peter and the Beloved Disciple that "they have taken the Lord from the tomb." Peter and this disciple race to the tomb. When the Beloved Disciple arrives first, he steps aside and allows Peter to enter, and they see the burial wrappings. They see and believe. Then comes the somewhat strange statement that "they did not yet understand the scripture that [Jesus] had to rise from the dead" (John 20:9). On first glance this seems almost like an anti-resurrection story: Mary thinks the body has been stolen; Peter and the Beloved Disciple do not really grasp the resurrection.

The Lectionary truncates John's resurrection account. In the rest of the story (John 20:11-18), Jesus first appears to the weeping Mary, who, like the woman of Canticles 2:9, is searching for her beloved. Jesus interrupts her search and asks the question which he posed to his first disciples (John 1:38), and which challenges us today: "What are you looking for?" Only when Jesus calls her by name (cf. John 10:3-5), "Mary," does she recognize him and call out with affection, "My teacher!" In an enigmatic sentence Jesus says, "Stop holding on to me, for I have not yet ascended to the Father" (John 20:17). Jesus then commissions her to proclaim this message "to my brothers," and, in the words of St. Bernard of Clairvaux, she becomes the *apostola apostolorum,* the "apostle to the apostles."

Clues to John's profound theology of the resurrection are scattered throughout. Mary and the Beloved Disciple arrive first at the tomb. In John love is the prime Christian virtue and the key to ultimate recognition of Jesus. Unlike Lazarus, who comes forth from the tomb clad in the burial cloths, Jesus' burial cloths are left behind. Christian faith is not belief in the resuscitation of the corpse but hope in a totally new kind of life. True resurrection faith does not arise from seeing and believing in an empty tomb but from meeting God in the Scriptures. When Jesus tells Mary, "Stop holding on," he says that though the earthly relationship is over, he will be with his loved ones in a totally new way.

Easter is really a total surprise; it does not fit in. Those who love Jesus are drawn to mourn his death, only to learn that he lives with them in a way that transcends their hopes. The death chamber becomes the door to life.

PRAYING WITH SCRIPTURE

- How can we affirm the victory of life over death in a culture in which deadly violence crouches at the schoolhouse door and death-dispensing poverty stunts young lives?

- When, like Mary, we feel that "they have taken my Lord," and we "don't know where they have laid him," can we hear again Jesus' words, "What are you looking for?" Can we hear him speak our baptismal name and follow his command to carry the Easter message to his brothers and sisters?

Second Sunday of Easter

Readings: Acts 4:32-35; Ps 118:2-4, 13-15, 22-24; 1 John 5:1-6;
John 20:19-31

> **"These things are written that you might come**
> **to believe" (John 20:31).**

Show Me!

In his important work, *The Sunday Lectionary* (The Liturgical Press, 1998), Normand Bonneau sketches the "architecture" of the readings for the Easter season, the fifty days from Easter to Pentecost, which focus on mystagogy, by which the newly baptized are led into a deeper understanding of their baptismal incorpation into Christ. The older designation "Sundays *after* Easter" yields to "Sundays *of* Easter," since each Sunday plays the resurrection message in a different key. There is no temporal sequence as in Advent or Lent, leading to the birth or the death of Jesus. Though the Easter season culminates in the celebration of the giving of the Spirit at Pentecost, in John the gift of the Spirit and sending of the disciples occur on the first Easter evening. Also, only during the Easter season are Old Testament readings omitted, to be replaced by readings from Acts, which stress the impact of the resurrection in the nascent Church. The gospels, apart from the Lukan appearance (third Sunday of Easter) are from John and contain memorable expressions of Jesus' care for and presence in the community (the Good Shepherd; the Vine and the Branches; the Love Command).

The gospel read today, once called "Sunday in White" to recall the day when the newly baptized doffed their white garments, recounts two appearances of the risen Jesus. On Easter evening the disciples are gathered in the darkness, fearful behind closed doors. The scene evokes the frequent association in John of darkness with lack of faith. Jesus' first word is "Peace," the biblical opposite of fear, not conflict, and a word that is closely associated with other biblical motifs such as justice, mercy, and loving kindness (Hos 2:22-23). Here and in the "doubting Thomas" incident, when Jesus shows his wounds his disciples recognize him. The symbolism is powerful. The risen Christ is the crucified one; Christ's presence among the community of believers is recognized by his wounds. This is the Johannine version of the Matthean presence of Christ in the suffering and marginal people of the world (Matt 25:31-46).

Jesus now includes the disciples in his own mission and fulfills his promise to send them the Holy Spirit (John 14:26-27), elsewhere called the Advocate (Paraclete, 16:7), or Spirit of truth (16:13). Recalling the original gift of life to Adam from God's breath, Jesus breathes on them and grants them the power over sins, to forgive or retain them (literally "hold" or "restrain"). Though later Church teaching sees this gift manifest in the sacrament of reconciliation, its original meaning is wider. The community of disciples is to be a community of forgiveness that sends sin away (the literal meaning of "forgive") and holds in check its destructive power.

The story of Thomas, set a week later, portrays an example of "unfaith," which seeks proof of the resurrection ("Do not be unbelieving"). Only after Jesus challenges him to touch his wounds does Thomas confess, "My Lord and my God." In words addressed to John's community and the Church through the ages, Jesus pronounces, "Blessed are those who have not seen but have believed," and the evangelist ends with a comment on the explicit purpose of the Gospel: it is written to bring people to faith in Jesus, the Messiah. Resurrection faith is the key to reading John's Gospel.

These readings, along with the passages from Acts and 1 John, offer a dense collection of motifs for prayer and preaching. By his resurrection Jesus fulfills his promise not to leave his followers orphans (John 14:18) and to bring them the fullness of joy (15:11). His followers share in the very same mission that he received from the Father. With the gift of the Spirit, a disciple of Jesus is to be the continuing presence of God's love in the world. Generations who walk in faith without "seeing" are "begotten of God" and more blessed than those who have seen and believed. This faith enables them to live as a community of "one heart and one mind," the classical description of friendship, which is cemented by concern for the poor and needy. The resurrection proclamation is not simply the victory over death or the promise of eternal life, but a summons to live as a community led by the Spirit, practicing forgiveness and resistance to evil, which takes shape in bonds of friendship that reach across the great economic divide between wealth and poverty.

PRAYING WITH SCRIPTURE

- Place yourself with the disciples, huddled in fear, and ask for that gift of joy and peace which the risen Christ can bring.

- Think of areas in which you are challenged to a forgiveness that manifests the presence of God's Spirit.

- Reflect on how the followers of Christ today still bear the wounds of the crucified one and pray that we may recognize the risen Christ in them.

- Pray about the wounds of Christ in the bodies of his followers, with the hope that we may come to see the risen Christ through their sufferings.

Third Sunday of Easter

Readings: Acts 3:13-15, 17-19; Ps 4:2, 4, 7-9; 1 John 2:1-5a;
Luke 24:35-48

> **"Know that the LORD does wonders**
> **for his faithful one" (Ps 4:4).**

REMEMBERING THE CHURCH'S FIRST COMMUNION

The readings continue to proclaim the reality and saving power of Christ's resurrection, while the gospel is the Lukan sequel to the meal of the risen Christ with the two travelers on the way to Emmaus (Luke 24:13-34). As in the Johannine Upper Room appearances, Jesus proclaims "Peace," shows his wounds, and the reality of bodily resurrection is affirmed by the meal he shares with his disciples (John 21:1-14), symbolizing that the Church will continue to experience Jesus' presence in its eucharistic gatherings.

Together with peace, forgiveness is one of the prime gifts of the risen Christ in both John and Luke. The Old Testament expressions for forgiveness image the removal or wiping away of an offense, with the added New Testament overtones of sending away the offense or release from a debt. The Bible stresses both divine and human forgiveness, epitomized in the Lord's Prayer, "Forgive us our debts (Luke 11:4, "sins") as we forgive our debtors (Matt 6:12).

Years ago Edward Schillebeeckx suggested that the appearances of the risen Jesus brought to the disciples a profound experience of forgiveness. All the Gospels depict the flight of the disciples and the denial of Peter. Paul was changed from persecutor to apostle by the grace of the risen Christ, and James, the brother of the Lord, who was not a follower of the earthly Jesus (Mark 3:20; 6:1-6), became a leader of the Jerusalem church. The peace that the risen Jesus brought was a release from the shame and failure of Jesus' first followers, which transformed them into missionaries and martyrs.

The gospel stresses that the disciples are to preach and to witness repentance and forgiveness to "all the nations." Zechariah had promised that the coming of Jesus would give his people "knowledge of salvation through the forgiveness of their sins" (Luke 1:77); the dying Jesus prays for forgiveness for his crucifiers (Luke 23:34); the mission of the risen Christ to his followers extends this forgiveness to all people.

Today forgiveness "to all nations" has moved from the religious and individual to the global political sphere. The Pope and bishops' conferences throughout the world call for forgiveness of international debts (*America,* March 25, 2000); Archbishop Desmond Tutu, after reviewing the work of the South African Truth and Reconciliation Commission, calls forgiveness absolutely necessary for continued human existence (*No Future Without Forgiveness,* [Doubleday, 1999]). After the breakup of the Soviet Union during the early stages of the conflicts in the former Yugoslavia, the novelist Mary Gordon wrote that "the heavy topsoil of repressed injustice breeds anger better than any other medium," and that anger "rolls and rolls like a flaming boulder down a hill gathering mass and speed," even when the original causes of the anger are forgotten. "The only way to stop this kind of irrational anger," she writes, "is by an act of equally irrational forgiveness" (*The New York Times Book Review,* June 13, 1993).

Recently the Church has moved from proclaiming the necessity of forgiveness to asking others to forgive those sufferings perpetrated by the very community that strives to embody the presence of the risen Christ. A frail and aging Pope kissing the feet of the crucifix or placing an apology in the Western Wall of the destroyed Temple symbolizes a sea change in the Church's witness to the nations.

Forgiveness permeates the other readings. Though God willed the rejection of the righteous one, God will wipe away sin (Acts 3:19), and 1 John states that we have an advocate, Jesus, who is expiation for our sin. Denial, rejection, sin are not the final word. The resurrection is victory over these deadly elements in life. Karl Rahner once wrote: "We are always tempted to stay in sin because we do not dare to believe in the magnificent love of God, and because we do not want to believe that God will forgive us our sins" (*The Content of Faith,* [Crossroad, 1993] p. 306). The experience of such love and irrational forgiveness touched the denying Peter, the doubting Thomas, and the fleeing disciples, and remains the enduring gift of the risen Christ to his followers.

PRAYING WITH SCRIPTURE

- At the eucharistic meal with the risen Christ, recall times when you have experienced God's surprising, forgiving love.

- Ask God for the grace to offer to others those irrational acts of forgiveness that may bring true Easter peace.

- Think of how your local parish or community may be a contemporary witness to forgiveness from God and with others.

Fourth Sunday of Easter

Readings: Acts 4:8-12; Ps 118:1, 8-9, 21-23, 26, 28, 29; 1 John 3:1-2;
John 10:11-18

"Beloved, we are God's children now" (1 John 3:2).

POOR LITTLE SHEEP WHO HAVE FOUND THE WAY

One of the most frequent subjects of early Christian art is Jesus the Good Shepherd, an image that often combines elements from the parable of the Lost Sheep (Luke 15:1-7) with Jesus' self-description in John 10. The beautiful fresco in Rome's catacomb of St. Domitilla is representative. In a setting of verdant growth, a young Jesus appears, a sheep draped around his shoulders, while other sheep look longingly at him, symbolizing that as Good Shepherd Christ will lead his followers to paradise.

The gospel for the fourth Sunday of Easter in all three cycles of the Lectionary readings is from the Johannine allegory of Jesus as both Door to the sheepfold and Shepherd (John 10). Then, until Pentecost, the gospels switch from appearances of the risen Jesus to selections from the farewell discourses in John 13 to 17. In the New Testament, especially in John, the passion, death, resurrection, and giving of the Spirit are one saving event, though they are played out over a period of time. In these parting words of Jesus to his earthy followers we hear the voice of the risen Jesus speaking to the Church through the ages.

Jesus twice describes himself as the Good Shepherd who knows the sheep and gives his life for them, in contrast to hirelings, who neglect the sheep. The translation "good" does not capture the nuance of the Greek, which suggests also an authentic or model shepherd. Behind the rich imagery of this passage are the frequent Old Testament uses of the shepherd image to describe God's care: for the people, important leaders in salvation history, Moses, David, anointed kings, and the hoped-for Messiah. Negatively, Jesus' contrast with the hirelings evokes God's polemic against false shepherds (leaders), who neglect the sheep and exploit them for their own gain (Ezek 34:11-31). It is unique to John that a messianic figure will give his life for the sheep. Though this anticipates Jesus' passion and death, the Greek expression, literally "put (or place) my life for the sake of others," implies that Jesus' whole life and teaching is a model for good shepherding.

With its references to "other sheep that do not belong to this fold," whom Jesus will also lead, and to the hope for "one flock, one shepherd," this gospel inspired Pope John XXIII's vision for the Second Vatican Council and has remained influential in ecumenical and interreligious dialogue. While "other sheep" in John is most likely a reference to the emerging Gentile mission, the expression has come to describe people who were not explicitly believers and yet remained touched in some mysterious sense by the grace of the Incarnation ("the Word became flesh," John 1:14), which affects all humanity. Too often, also, the "one flock and one shepherd" are envisioned in ecclesial or structural terms. Its background is Jewish hopes that at the endtime the Messiah would unify all the scattered people of Israel and gather the "nations" to Zion. In John it also evokes a future hope ("there will be") of final unity in Christ. This is willed by God and is a goal that should shape Church life and teaching, but it is ultimately God's doing. Throughout history a Church that listens to the voice of the risen Jesus is to be one of service and mutual, self-giving love as an authentic witness to the sheep not of this fold.

This Sunday is also designated World Day of Prayer for Vocations, so one immediately thinks of the wide range of vocations to "pastoral service," lay, religious, and priestly. Yet the readings warn against identifying too readily "office" with pastoral ministry. Jesus is the Shepherd who knows the sheep, and they will hear his voice. This passage foreshadows John's version of the Petrine ministry (John 21:15-19), when Peter, who denied Jesus three times, is drawn to affirm his love three times and is only then commissioned to feed and care for "my sheep." Unlike Matthew 16:16-18, there is no commission to exercise authoritative power. During this Eastertide the Church is reminded of Jesus, who conquered death, who will lead his sheep to paradise, and who is a model of authentic pastoral care defined in terms of knowing and self-emptying service, which extends to the other sheep who "do not belong to this fold."

Praying with Scripture

- Pray quietly with the biblical "shepherd" passages: Psalm 23, Ezekiel 34; Micah 5:3-5; Jeremiah 23:1-4; Luke 15:1-7. What deep feelings do these evoke? How can these texts touch your life?

- Gandhi was inspired by the figure of Jesus. Think of and pray in gratitude for those other sheep, not of this fold, who hear and model the teaching of Jesus.

- Reflect on the many ways in which lives are placed at the service of others: parents' care of children; acts of kindness to co-workers; compassion for those who are "like sheep without a shepherd" (Mark 6:34).

Fifth Sunday of Easter

Readings: Acts 9:26-31; Ps 22:26-28, 30-32; 1 John 3:18-24;
John 15:1-8

"Remain in me, as I remain in you" (John 15:4).

A LOVE SONG FOR GOD'S VINEYARD

A frequent question these days is, "Just what does it mean to be a Christian?" The readings this Sunday and next provide a powerful answer. The gospels, taken from John 15, use the symbol of the vine and the branches to describe the intimate union between Christ and the believer. This begins with God's initiative, is sealed by Christ's death, and is expressed in love of God and neighbor, which resounds through the second readings from 1 John. Simply put, to be a Christian is to live united with God in Christ, expressed in love for God and others.

The vine is one of the most powerful biblical images for God's relation to the people. Israel is the vine brought out of Egypt and a choice vine planted by God (Ps 80:8; Jer 2:21). She is also a vineyard planted and tended by God (Isa 5:1-7; 27:3). Jesus builds on this image by calling himself the "true" Vine and his Father the Vinegrower. This image is profound, since the vine and the branches (unlike a tree trunk and the limbs) are often virtually indistinguishable, and since there is a mutual interchange of life between them.

John 15 is also characterized by one of the most distinctive Johannine theological concepts, "abiding" (NAB, "remain," also translated as "stay"), which appears over forty times in that Gospel. Characteristic of John is that terms from daily life—such as *remain, light, water, darkness, walk*—take on profound symbolic meanings, which invite readers constantly to ponder their depth. Early in the Gospel, when Jesus asks the disciples, "What do you seek," they counter with "Where are you staying?" and then they stay with him. People brought to Jesus by the Samaritan woman "remain" with Jesus two days. Discipleship in John begins with brief "abiding" with Jesus, walks the walk of his life, and culminates in the symbol of the branches abiding in the vine.

The union between Christ and the believer is vividly described by Paul and John. Paul speaks over one hundred sixty times of being "in Christ" and uses the metaphor of the body: "All the parts of the body, though many, are one body, so also Christ" (1 Cor 12:12). But John's metaphor suggests a more intimate union. "Unlike Paul's image of the body and its members which is invoked in 1 Corinthians 12 to accommodate the multitude of charisms, the Johannine image of the vine and the branches places emphasis on only one issue: dwelling on the vine or inherence in Jesus" (Raymond E. Brown, *Journal of Biblical Literature*, 97:5-22). Such a close union between Jesus and the believer is not the privileged experience of saints and mystics alone; for John it is the core of Christian life.

The vine must be both nurtured and pruned, symbolizing perhaps the inevitable suffering of the disciples in imitation of Jesus. The vines must bear fruit that will lead to full discipleship, and unfruitful vines wither and are used only for firewood. This reflects the double image of the vine/vineyard in the Old Testament. Despite the tender care the vineyard owner (God) lavished on the vineyard in Isaiah 5, sadly it yields the wild grapes of bloodshed rather than justice, and outcries rather than righteousness. Jesus' abiding presence is not static but must be nurtured, and it can wither. Not even John's great vision of the union of God and humanity takes away the mystery of human freedom and the need to grow in responsive love. The reading from 1 John tells us simply what fruit we must bear: "Let us love not in word or speech but in deed and truth" (1 John 3:18); and the truth is that whenever our hearts condemn us, "God is greater than our hearts" (1 John 3:20).

The Easter season celebrates the abiding presence of the risen Christ. Yet, for Catholics in the United States the readings may seem unrealistic. We are doers, act-ers, and we like quickly to translate the gospel vision into deeds. John provides us with a profound challenge—to stop, to "abide" with Jesus, to realize God's presence. Often I think of two human analogies to John's "abiding": one from life in its fullness and one from early life on the brink of growth. For people in a long, loving, fruitful marriage, often mere presence is enough; few words are needed, but when one leaves, even for a short time, the other's eyes turn frequently to the door. The two have become one flesh—and one heart and spirit. This is the Johannine "abiding." Last Christmas I watched my fifteen-year-old grandniece, a young woman of wonderful energy and full of life, yet she could "hang out" with her best friend, spending hours together, often listening to music, sometimes talking, other times just sitting. Perhaps our culture should learn how to "hang out" with Jesus.

PRAYING WITH SCRIPTURE

- Sit simply and quietly with the risen Christ, conscious that every breath you take is a sign of the Spirit's presence.

- Jesus says that the fruit of remaining in him is that "whatever you want, it will be done for you." Place before God your "wants," hopes, and fears.

- John states that we should have confidence whenever our hearts condemn us, for God is greater than our hearts. Pray about ways that God's love is greater than the indictments of our hearts.

Sixth Sunday of Easter

Readings: Acts 10:25-26, 34-35, 44-48; Ps 98:1-4; 1 John 4:7-10;
John 15:9-17

> **"Whoever is without love does not know God,**
> **for God is love" (1 John 4:8).**

WHERE CAN YOU FIND TRUE FRIENDSHIP?

Three years ago *Nothing Sacred*, a warm and sympathetic television series about the lives of priests, religious, and people in an urban parish, was canceled near the end of its first season. Various reasons were bandied about—broadsides from the Catholic League for Religious and Civil Rights, overly sophisticated content, the fact that it aired at the same time as the immensely popular sitcom *Friends.* Rather ironically, *Friends*, a procession of mindless episodes parading six urban yuppies facing trivial problems has very little to do with real friendship, while *Nothing Sacred* was all about the kind of friendship Jesus speaks about in today's gospel—mutual affection, crossing barriers, and putting one's life at the service of others.

The gospel continues the exhortation "to abide," simply stated: "remain in my love." In John a command is always based on a prior experience of grace, so Jesus says simply, "love one another as I love you," and then points to the summit of love, laying down one's life for friends. This part of the farewell discourse clearly echoes Jesus' words and actions at the Last Supper, when he washes his disciples' feet as an example and first gives them the new commandment that they love and serve "one another as I love you" (John 15:12). The little "as" underscores one of the deepest Johannine insights. The immense gift of love precedes and makes possible discipleship. The second reading captures this perfectly: "In this is love: not that we have loved God, but that he loved us and sent his Son as expiation for our sins" (1 John 4:10).

Jesus then goes on to call his disciples friends. John's readers would immediately recognize friendship as the highest form of love, expressed by popular Hellenistic sayings such as "friends hold all things in common," or "friends are other selves," or "friends share a single soul" (cf. Acts 2:44; 4:32). Communality of heart and soul united early Christians. Friendship was expressed through hospitality, shared meals, and bearing one another's burdens (Gal 6:2). Jesus calls his disciples no longer slaves but friends, since the brutal institution of slavery was rarely bridged even by friendship. Jesus' act of footwashing, in which he assumed the role of the slave, was a symbol of his love, which bridged this gap and liberated the disciples. Paul expresses the same vision of friendship when he expects Jew and Greek, slave and free, male and female to form a new bonding in Christ (Gal 3:28). The Johannine Jesus bridges a gap even wider than slavery—the gap between the divine and the human. No followers of his are ever again to think of God as "master" and see themselves as slaves. They are friends.

As we near the end of Eastertide and prepare for the great cycle of feasts from Ascension through Pentecost to Corpus Christi, we might pause to ask whether our Church can truly go out and bear fruit. Polarization continues to divide the Church and is often a scandal to authentic witness. Endless discussion about differences and their sources will do little to bridge such polarization, but a deep realization of the pregnant word "as" may call both sides up short. Without a deep experience of the self-emptying love of Christ, who summons us to be friends, withered branches will continue to blight the vine.

Praying with Scripture

- Recall in grateful prayer experiences of deep friendship and pray about Jesus' words, "I have called you friends."

- Pray in gratitude for the experience of "as," when God's love liberated you to build bridges to others.

The Ascension of the Lord

Readings: Acts 1:1-11; Ps 47:2-3, 6-9; Eph 1:17-23 or 4:1-13;
Mark 16:15-20

"The Lord worked with them" (Mark 16:20).

Today's feast follows the Lukan picture of the exaltation of Jesus. Only Luke has a forty-day schema followed by Pentecost, and while the day is called the Ascension of the Lord, the focus of the readings is on the exaltation of Jesus, who commissions his followers to carry on his mission. The Church, like the disciples, is not to stand "looking intently at the sky" but to carry on Jesus' mission to the ends of the earth.

This appears dramatically in the reading from Ephesians, which begins with the ringing exhortation to the seven unities—one body, one spirit, one hope, one Lord, one faith, one baptism, one God and Father of all—that have motivated ecumenical movements from the beginning.

The ascension of Jesus is the reason that the exalted Jesus, like an enthroned monarch, can dispense gifts. These gifts are then the different offices and ministries given to the Church, which Ephesians expresses in an important manner: "And he gave some as apostles, others as prophets, others as evangelists, others as pastors and teachers, *to equip the holy ones for the work of ministry,* for the building up of the body of Christ, until we all attain the unity of faith" (Eph 4:11-12).

In contrast to some earlier translations, the work of ministry is the mission of "all the saints," and the function of the offices, prophets, etc., is *to equip* them for this work. This section of Ephesians should permeate all discussion of mission and ministry today.

PRAYING WITH SCRIPTURE

- Pray quietly over the seven unities and think of how we build up the body of Christ and advance toward the unity of faith.

- Reflect on the variety of ministries in the Church and how you have been or may be called to a special ministry.

Seventh Sunday of Easter

Readings: Acts 1:15-17, 20a, 20c-26; Ps 103:1-2, 11-12, 19-20;
1 John 4:11-16; John 17:11-19

"Consecrate them in truth. Your word is truth"
(John 17:17).

JESUS' LAST WILL AND TESTAMENT

The first reading captures the meaning of today's liturgical celebration. Matthias, not one of the original followers of Jesus, is chosen to be "a witness to the resurrection." From Easter to Pentecost all the readings in effect present different aspects of what it means to be such a witness.

The gospel concludes the Johannine farewell discourses with a selection from "the Testament of Jesus," or "his high priestly prayer," which comprises one long prayer to his Father, so powerful and so poignant that it should be read in its entirety. The Lectionary excerpt is poorly chosen, since the prayer has three units: Jesus' prayer for himself (17:1-5), for his disciples (vv. 6-19), and for future believers (vv. 20-26). Among non-biblical Jewish writings slightly earlier or contemporary with the New Testament, there is a collection called *Testaments of the Twelve Patriarchs*, or of Moses, narratives of the deaths of the great founding figures of Israel. These bid farewell to their loved ones, speaking of how God touched their lives and warning them of dangers they face. This literary genre has clearly influenced John 17. We are invited to listen as Jesus, whose death is imminent, gives voice to his deepest hopes for his loved ones.

Jesus prays that the disciples may experience that unity he shares with his Father, that they may share in his joy, and that they will be consecrated in truth. Jesus also prays for their protection in a hostile world. His own life is a paradigm for the lives of believers. He comes from above, from presence with God, to an alien world that does not accept him, and then returns to the Father. The believer, in John, is born from above (1:12-13; 3:3), lives in a hostile and alien world (15:18-19; 16:33; 17:14, 16, 18); and, as Jesus returns to the Father, the destiny of his followers is to be with him (12:26; 14:2-3, 13).

The ambiguity of "the world" echoes throughout John. It was made "through him" (the Word) but did not recognize him (1:10-11). Jesus takes away the sin of the world, and God so loved the world that he gave his only Son; he is the living Bread that will be the life of the world (6:51). Yet "the world" often symbolizes the power of evil organized against Jesus and his followers (see especially 3:19; 15:18-19). Though other New Testament writings have a more positive attitude toward the world, and though the contemporary Church is summoned to be engaged in the world and to discern the manifestations of goodness among non-Christians, in John, Jesus and the disciples come to the world not to change it but to challenge its values. The mission should not be lost amid the contemporary change of attitude.

Jesus asks his Father also to consecrate them (literally "make holy") "in truth." Holiness in the Bible is not primarily a moral category but is a way of speaking about living in the presence of God. It is more similar to a "zone" or "marked-off area," than a personal disposition. Disciples are to operate in this zone, which is also "in truth." The Greek term for "truth," *alētheia,* means "unconcealment" or "revelation," removal of a veil, and in John refers principally to the unveiling or revelation of God in the life and teaching of Jesus (1:14, 17; 14:6, "I am the truth"). Jesus prays that the disciples will live in a zone of God's presence (holiness) as they faithfully witness to the truth of his life.

The readings this Sunday before Pentecost provide a bridge between the continued celebration of the resurrection and yearning for God's Spirit, which will come only after the departure of Jesus. Jesus' prayer anticipates the coming of the Spirit of truth (14:7; 15:26). Today this final wish of Jesus that his Father make the Church holy in truth has a dramatic relevance. The last decade has been marked by deplorable accounts of sexual and financial abuse in the Church. People are often most scandalized, not only by the sins themselves but by an unwillingness to face the truth, often "killing the messenger," or by feeble cover-ups (the direct opposite of "unveil").

At the same time hopeful signs emerge of truth-filled living in a zone of holiness, such as the profoundly moving service of healing and reconciliation for victims of clergy abuse held by the diocese of Oakland and presided over by Bishop John S. Cummins, who offered an honest apology and asked for "pardon and forgiveness." Such is the kind of holiness and witness that Jesus, on the brink of death, prayed to his Father to grant his followers.

Praying with Scripture

- Place yourself in a circle with Jesus' disciples and read slowly John 17, asking how this is also a prayer for you.

- In the second reading we hear, "Beloved, if God so loved us, we also must love one another." Pray this verse almost like a mantra, letting it sink deeply into your hearts.

- Pray about ways that all in the Church may better live out their consecration in truth.

The Mystery of Faith Twice Renewed
Pentecost Sunday

Readings: Acts 2:1-11; Ps 104:1, 24, 29-30, 31, 34; 1 Cor 12:3b-7,
12-13 or Gal 5:16-25; John 20:19-23 or John 15:26-27; 16:12-15

"When you send forth your Spirit, they are created,
and you renew the face of the earth" (Ps 104:30).

A LIVING GOD PRESENT IN SPIRIT AND POWER

Pentecost, traditionally called "the birthday of the Church," concludes the Lent-Easter season, as the Church returns to Ordinary Time.
Profound theological insights cluster around the feast and its readings.
Though originally a Jewish spring harvest festival, the Feast of Weeks,
celebrated fifty days after Passover, it gradually developed into commemoration of the Sinai covenant. In Luke's theology the Twelve, the
nucleus of God's renewed people of the "new covenant in my blood"
(Luke 22:20), receive the promised "power from on high" (Luke 24:49)
by the descent of God's Spirit, which enables them to proclaim the message of the Resurrection. The Spirit becomes the energizing presence as
the Church moves outward to the ends of the earth, breaking through
geographical and ethnic boundaries.

The narrative from Acts, in which the disciples, speaking their own
language, are understood by people representing the geographical
boundaries of the known world, also presents a reversal of the confu-
sion of tongues at the tower of Babel. When humans raise themselves
up to God to "make a name" for themselves, they are dispersed and
confused in language. When God's Spirit comes down upon them, divisions are broken down. This remains a particular mandate for the
contemporary Church in an increasingly fragmented world.

The gospel recalls Jesus' promise that after his departure he will send
an advocate, a spirit of truth (also called the Holy Spirit, 14:26) that will
bear witness to himself. The Greek term translated "Paraclete" has

many overtones, suggesting a legal advocate as well as a helper and one who offers consolation (see 2 Cor 1:3-7). This Advocate will continue the work of Jesus by bearing witness to him, teaching the disciples and bringing to remembrance the teaching of Jesus (John 14:25-26). Like Jesus, the Advocate will not be received by "the world" (14:16). Simply put, the Spirit is the continuing presence of the Christ-event in the world.

The readings offer directions for proclaiming the presence of the Spirit in the Church. Often this is associated with the "enthusiastic" phenomena of inspired speech or other charismatic gifts like healing. At other times the Holy Spirit is seen as a behind-the-scenes "fixer" of questionable actions or decisions in the Church—"Well, the Holy Spirit knows what he is doing"; "Just trust the Holy Spirit; it will work out." John's theology qualifies such views. The life and teaching of Jesus is the criterion of the presence of the Spirit of Truth who brings to remembrance the Way, the Truth and the Life. The Pauline reading conveys a similar perspective: the fruit of the Spirit is seen in acts of love, joy, kindness, and generosity. When actions are done in fidelity to the example of Jesus and produce such fruits, the Spirit of Truth is present. Such is the challenge of Pentecost to the Church.

PRAYING WITH SCRIPTURE

(See Solemnity of the Most Holy Trinity.)

Sunday after Pentecost
The Solemnity of the Most Holy Trinity

Readings: Deut 4:32-34, 39-40; Ps 33:4-6, 9, 18-20, 22; Rom 8:14-17; Matt 28:16-20

"For you did not receive a spirit of slavery to fall back into fear, but you received a Spirit of adoption" (Rom 8:15).

SHARING IN THE VERY LIFE OF GOD

During the time of theological ferment following the Second Vatican Council, I overheard a conversation between two older Jesuits. One was upset over reports of new thinking on the Trinity. After some time, the other said, "Well, can you still pray to the Trinity?" The response was: "No way. I have always been a Jesus man, myself."

The Trinity presents a series of paradoxes. It is the central mystery of Christian faith, yet its power in Christian life gets lost amid a tangle of theological distinctions and philosophical speculation. The Trinity reveals the God who is the ground and center of our lives, yet often seems distant from daily Christian life and is one of the most difficult mysteries to preach on.

Today's readings present rich material for prayer and preaching. Moses, who had experienced the mystery of God at the burning bush (Exod 3:1-6), states the foundation of all Trinitarian thinking: there is one God, who is both transcendent and deeply involved in the life of the people. The final words of Matthew's Gospel commission the disciples to make disciples by baptizing people in the name of the Father and of the Son and of the Holy Spirit. "In the name of" suggests participation in the very life of God, and Paul makes the extraordinary statement that those who are led by God's Spirit become sons and daughters of God and joint heirs with Christ. The oft-cited phrase of Cyril of Alexandria comes to mind: "We become by grace what God is by nature."

As the late Catherine LaCugna, whose early death deprived the Church of a major theological voice, stressed in her landmark work, *God For Us: The Trinity in Christian Life* (HarperSanFrancisco, 1991), the Trinity reveals that the transcendent God who is beyond words and definitions is disclosed in the life, teaching, death and resurrection of Jesus and continues as Spirit to empower and guide the Church. Matthew's disciples are instructed not only to baptize but to "teach them [the nations] to observe all that I have commanded you." The Trinity is about a God for us, who lived as a blessing for the poor and mourners, confronted the power of evil, entered with compassion into the world of human suffering, broke down the barriers between human sin and divine holiness and reconciled enemies. The pattern of Jesus' life manifests the triune God who is "with us" until the end of the age.

PRAYING WITH SCRIPTURE

- Read prayerfully the Pauline readings for the feasts of Pentecost and the Trinity, reflecting on how our adoption into the very life of God brings forth fruits of love, joy, peace, patience, kindness, generosity, faithfulness, gentleness, and self-control.

- Pray about ways in which the Spirit is leading the Church today to break down barriers that separate people and nations.

- Making the sign of the cross, pray often to God who is Father bringing forth life in love and freedom, Son living and dying for others, and Spirit teaching and empowering a Church to be God's very presence in the world.

The Solemnity of the
Most Holy Body and Blood of Christ

Readings: Exod 24:3-8; Ps 116:12-13, 15-18; Heb 9:11-15;
Mark 14:12-16, 22-26

**"The cup of salvation I will take up,
and I will call upon the name of the LORD" (Ps 116:12).**

A PEOPLE OF THE COVENANT

Two themes echo throughout the readings: covenant and sacrifice. Exodus recounts the ratification of the Sinai covenant by a sacrificial ritual in which the people affirm the whole content of Exodus 19–24, proclaiming "all that the LORD has said, we will heed and do" (Exod 24:7). The Letter to the Hebrews presents a Christian interpretation of the ritual for the Day of Atonement (Lev 16), stressing that Jesus is "mediator of a new covenant." The gospel roots this in the final Passover meal of Jesus with his disciples, in which Jesus offers his body and his "blood of the covenant, which will be shed for many."

Covenant is one of the major theological ideas of the Old Testament. It has its roots in agreements made in the ancient Near East between peoples that created peace through the enchange of promises of shared obligations and respect. The Sinai covenant recalls God's rescue of the people from slavery (Exod 19:4-6), and the people respond by committing themselves to God's Torah or way of acting as a grateful and liberated people. God's gift precedes God's commands.

Covenants were ratified often by sacrifices, which symbolized the total commitment of the partners and often concluded with a meal during which the offering was consumed, symbolizing that the commitments affirmed would continue to nurture the people. In the New Testament Jesus becomes both the one who enacts the new covenant and the one who offers his whole life (body and blood) as a covenant meal. Eating the body and drinking the blood of Christ is a commitment to be nurtured by the kind and quality of life embodied by Jesus of Nazareth. As the early Jerusalem Catechesis states, "His body is given to us under the symbol of bread, and his blood is given to us under the symbol of wine, in order to make us by receiving them one body and one blood with him" (Office of Readings for the Saturday after Easter).

The readings remind us of those covenants that shape our Christian lives. All the sacraments are covenants in which the initiative comes from God and the commitments are to be lived out by those who "affirm" or receive the sacraments. Marriage is perhaps the best human analogue to biblical covenants. People who have experienced already the gift of mutual love, give to each other their whole selves, as Jesus gave his body and blood for those he loved. The sacrifice offered by Jesus and enacted at every celebration of the Eucharist is also a reminder that Christian life, and especially marriage, is sacrificial as ordinary existence is transformed into something holy, which is experienced by self-giving "in good times and in bad, in sickness and in health."

PRAYING WITH SCRIPTURE

- Pray for the grace to realize that by receiving the body and blood of Christ we become members of Christ and of each other.

- In the quiet moments following the reception of the Eucharist, offer a prayer of thanksgiving to the "Son of God who has loved me and given himself up for me" (Gal 2:19).

June 29

SS. Peter and Paul, Apostles

Readings: Acts 12:1-10; Ps 34:2-9; 2 Tim 4:6-8, 17-19; Matt 16:13-19

> **We honor your great apostles:**
> **Peter, our leader in the faith, and Paul,**
> **its fearless preacher (Preface for the feast).**

AN ANCIENT LEGACY, AN ENDURING MISSION

Today's feast, one of the most ancient in the Church, celebrates the apostolic careers and martyrdom of two great missionaries of the early Church. In the East it was celebrated as early as the fourth century, but usually very close to Christmas, often on December 28. At Rome, as early as A.D. 258, the feast was celebrated *ad catacumbas* ("in the catacombs") on the Appian Way.

Persecution and divine rescue permeate the readings. The reading from Acts recounts the miraculous rescue of Peter from prison after the martyrdom of James (son of Zebedee) during the persecution under Herod Agrippa, while in the second reading Paul, knowing that his life is being poured out like a libation, praises and thanks God for rescuing him from the lion's mouth and for letting him proclaim the Gospel to the Gentiles. The gospel contains the promise to Peter that he will be a "rock" who will withstand persecution and that he will be given the power of the keys and the power to bind and loose (which later, in Matthew 18:16, will be given to the larger community).

Especially since the First Vatican Council, the Matthean text has been at the center of the understanding of the Petrine ministry and the basis of *ex cathedra* infallible teaching and universal jurisdiction. Yet the dogmatic definition does not exhaust the richness of Matthew's text. Important in Matthew is the gratuitous revelation to Peter that Jesus is Messiah and Son of God. Throughout Matthew's Gospel, Peter is one with little faith who often doubts and even fails but is rescued by the action of Jesus (14:28; 17:24-27). Jesus also stresses that on Peter the rock, he will build *his church,* which will be stronger than the forces of evil. Throughout Church history "the rock" has been variously interpreted. The early "typological" and "mother" of all interpretations was that Peter is the symbol of every true, spiritual Christian on whom the Church is built (Origen).

Strong in the Middle Ages was the interpretation that "this rock" was Christ himself. Likewise, the power of the keys has been interpreted from rabbinical writings as the power to impose or remove a binding decision (the current ecclesiological understanding), along with the power to exclude people from the community (Matt 18:18). Some scholars have also suggested that the promise contains overtones of "binding up" the power of evil and "loosening" people from sin.

While this section of Matthew has been a rich source for understanding the Petrine ministry, it has caused suffering and division. In his landmark encyclical "On Commitment to Ecumenism" (*Ut Unum Sint,* May 25, 1996), Pope John Paul II stated that "the Catholic Church's conviction that in the ministry of the Bishop of Rome she has preserved, in fidelity to the Apostolic Tradition and the faith of the Fathers, the visible sign and guarantor of unity, constitutes a difficulty for most other Christians, whose memory is marked by certain painful recollections." The Pope then added the following memorable statement: "To the extent that we are responsible for these, I join my Predecessor Paul VI in asking forgiveness." The Pope goes on to mention those New Testament passages which speak of the weakness of both Peter and Paul (e.g., Luke 22:31-32; John 15-19; 2 Cor 12:9-10) which "show that the Church is founded upon the infinite power of grace." Pope John Paul II then envisions a Petrine ministry characterized by mercy and a desire for unity.

Though the liturgy seems to focus more on Peter than on Paul, it is their mutual yet distinct roles that are celebrated. Paul, a person of great energy and passion, is called, like the prophet Jeremiah, to proclaim the love and mercy of God manifest in the cross of Christ. He nurtures his communities with a mother's love and encourages and guides them like a father (1 Thess 2:7, 11), yet he reacts with a violent outburst, hoping that those who attack the freedom of the Gospel "might also castrate themselves" (Gal 5:12). Though he recognizes that Peter was the first to see the risen Lord, he does not hesitate to criticize him for duplicity: "When Cephas came to Antioch, I opposed him to his face because he clearly was wrong" (Gal 2:11).

As we celebrate this feast today of "the princes of the apostles," we recall the legacy handed down to be a Church of apostles and martyrs. We celebrate the gift of the Petrine ministry as a witness of leadership and unity for the Churches today, while not forgetting the prophetic witness of Paul. Can the Petrine ministry reach its fullness without a Paul to challenge it? Paul and Peter died most likely during the persecution under Nero about A.D. 67. Following different courses in life, they join in death as models for us of the cost and glory of following Christ.

PRAYING WITH SCRIPTURE

- In *Ut Unum Sint* the Pope says that the Church of God is called to "manifest to a world ensnared by its sins and evil designs that, despite everything, God in his mercy can convert hearts to unity and enable them to enter into communion with him." Let this become our prayer.

- Pray for those today who give their lives as a cost of proclaiming and living the Gospel.

Fourteenth Sunday in Ordinary Time

Readings: Ezek 2:2-5; Ps 123:1-4; 2 Cor 12:7-10; Mark 6:1-6

**"My grace is sufficient for you,
for power is made perfect in weakness" (2 Cor 12:7).**

You Can't Go Home Again, Yeshua

The prophetic life is a strong theme in the readings for the next two weeks. God's spirit enters Ezekiel, and he is summoned to preach to rebellious people. Jesus returns to his hometown, is rejected by his family, and proclaims, "A prophet is not without honor except in his native place and among his own kin and in his own house." Today, when prophecy is more associated with sectarian and often destructive religious visionaries, its biblical meaning must be recovered. The term comes from the Greek, *prophētēs*—literally, one who speaks "on behalf of." A prophet speaks on behalf of God, as God's messenger and on behalf of those who have no one to speak for them, giving a voice to the voiceless (for example, the widow, the orphan, the poor, the stranger in the land). A prophet is not primarily a fore-teller, but a forth-teller, who proclaims with insight the evils that afflict society and can ultimately spell its downfall, as Jeremiah warned against political entanglements that led to the Babylonian exile. Prophets are "radical" in the sense that they reach back into the deepest roots of a religious tradition and summon people to be faithful to them, as the Hebrew prophets evoke the exile from Egypt and the Sinai covenant.

Today's gospel provides a window into the life of the pre-Easter Jesus. He was a prophet who proclaimed the nearness of God's reign, urged people to take a second look at their lives (Mark 1:14-15), and embodied God's mercy by associating with the marginal and suspect people of his day. Jesus' rejection by his family, recounted earlier in Mark (3:20-21; 31-35), is mentioned by all the Gospels. None of the named relatives of Jesus were among his first disciples, and only John reports that his mother is at the cross. Why did Jesus' relatives and townsfolk reject him? He is called "a carpenter," a somewhat derogatory term for one who claims to teach God's word. The names of his "brothers"—James, Joses (shortened form of Joseph), Judas, and Simon—recall leading figures of Israel's history. Jesus probably did not fulfill their hopes for a nationalistic messiah (see Luke 24:21; Acts 1:6) but proclaimed instead forgiveness of enemies and acceptance of the Gentiles. He teaches in the synagogue, but his teaching shocks his hearers; they cannot figure him out. His understanding of God and God's action does not fit into their categories. Because of their closed minds, "he was not able to perform any mighty deed there."

Today's readings remind the Church of the risk of silencing the voice of prophecy. In the 1940s Jesuits were forced to leave some university communities because of their outspoken criticism of racism. As I write these lines, television is filled with stories of the twenty-fifth anniversary of the end of the Vietnam war. There were no stories of David Miller, who burned his draft card in protest in 1966, or of the opposition of Dorothy Day and others who spoke out when the U.S. bishops issued their 1966 statement, "Peace and Vietnam," saying that U.S. action in Vietnam was justified, a position adamantly supported by Francis Cardinal Spellmann until the bitter end. Today the Church must ask what prophetic voices are not held in honor as people often ask, "What kind of wisdom has been given them?" (cf. Mark 6:2). As the Church summons us to repentance for sins of the past, who, like Ezekiel, will call us to task for our present sins?

PRAYING WITH SCRIPTURE

- Pray in gratitude for people who have influenced your life by giving you insight into God's will and by speaking out for those who have no voice.

- Read prayerfully 2 Cor 12:7-10, recalling difficult times when God's grace sustained you.

Fifteenth Sunday in Ordinary Time

Readings: Amos 7:12-15; Ps 85:9-14; Eph 1:3-14; Mark 6:7-13

"Off with you, visionary, flee to the land of Judah!" (Amos 7:12).

No Carry-Ons Allowed

The readings plunge us into the middle of a shouting match. Amaziah, a priest of the royal shrine of Bethel in Israel (the northern kingdom), is throwing out Amos, a Judean prophet, telling him to go home and make a living. Amos replies that he is no prophet, that is, no court prophet in employ of the king, but a shepherd and farmer, called by God to "prophesy to my people Israel." The gospel passage follows immediately the story of Jesus' rejection as a "prophet without honor," who then commissions his twelve disciples to adopt the prophetic lifestyle of itinerant preachers.

In Mark the "formation" of the disciples unfolds in stages. They are called to follow Jesus and become people who fish for humans (1:16-20); later they are called "to be with him" and are given power over evil (3:13-19). At this point their mission closely parallels that of Jesus: preaching repentance, confronting the power of evil, healing the sick. Jesus will later tell them that they too will be rejected by their loved ones (13:9-13).

The lack of material support, food, money, and sack (briefcase), and their dependence on hospitality from others are signs of their total reliance on God and of their freedom. Unlike Amaziah, they are not prophets for hire. Shaking the dust from one's feet was a symbolic act that the Jews performed when leaving a pagan or unclean land. The disciples are to symbolize to those who do not welcome them that they are subject to God's judgment.

This lifestyle seems strange and even harsh to us today, and it was not really normative even in the early Church. Still, it has lasting value.

First the Twelve are to re-present in their lives the actions of Jesus, even though Jesus is not with them. Today people often ask where Jesus is amid disputes over authority in the Church, endless meetings, and projects for renewal, or escalating signs of wealth and prestige. Yet people like Dorothy Day, Mother Teresa, or Jean Vanier traveled light and made people ask where Jesus is truly found. The rejection of the disciples and the advice simply to continue to other places reminds the Church that certain approaches may be fruitless, that it is time to move on. Though thrown out of the shrine, Amos moves on and delivers his strongest denunciations of those who "trample on the needy and bring the poor of the land to ruin" (Amos 8:4). Awareness of God's call, traveling light, and risking rejection—these are the "carry-ons" for true prophets.

PRAYING WITH SCRIPTURE

- Pray about times when your deepest religious commitments may have brought conflict or misunderstanding even with family and loved ones.

- In our contemporary culture of material excess, pray about ways that we, as a community of disciples, may travel light.

Sixteenth Sunday in Ordinary Time

Readings: Jer 23:1-6; Ps 23:1-6; Eph 2:13-18; Mark 6:30-34

"I will appoint shepherds for them who will shepherd them so that they need no longer fear and tremble" (Jer 23:4).

SHEPHERDS NEEDED

The father of a close Jesuit friend died shortly before Easter. A parade example of "the greatest generation," he had lived a full, dedicated and colorful life, which had been captured in taped recollections by his adult grandchildren and encapsulated in an obituary. When he was a teenager near Rapid City, South Dakota, every summer he would go into the mountains to give his uncle Joe, a shepherd, a chance to come to town for his "annual" bath and shave (he said that the uncle had grown to look like the sheep). Once his uncle gave him a .45 pistol to protect the sheep, which he fired out of curiosity only to have the sheep scatter in all directions. It took half a day to round them up again. He certainly learned that sheep need prudent care and protection.

Images from the world of shepherds characterize today's readings. The gospel recounts the return of the disciples from their missionary journey (Mark 6:7-13), and Jesus invites them to come away to a "deserted" place for rest, which ends up being short-lived as crowds stream out and arrive before them. Jesus then is moved with pity for them (literally "has compassion on"), for they were "like sheep without a shepherd," and he then teaches them. This brief description is dense with biblical allusions. Like the people of Israel, the crowds are in the desert, where they will receive not only miraculous food (next Sunday's gospel) but guidance and instruction, just as the Torah was given in the desert of Sinai.

In the Lectionary context, Jesus is to represent that good shepherd promised in Jeremiah, who will shepherd the sheep "so that they need no longer fear and tremble." He will also be a Davidic king who shall do what is just and right in the land. Inevitably also Christian readers think of Jesus as the shepherd of Psalm 23.

Throughout Church history, "pastoring" (shepherding) has been a prime image for leadership and care, and today "pastoral" ministry includes not only those named or ordained as "pastors" but many who follow different calls to serve and lead others. The readings may offer a handy job description. The pastor must be a person of compassion, which is the ability to feel deeply the suffering of others, to understand why they fear and tremble. And yet pastors are called to lead and "govern wisely" (Jer 23:5), living the teaching they communicate. They are to guide people in right paths and to be concerned about what is right and just in the land. Here is the continuing mandate to the Church to be a voice for justice in the world. Finally, all the images convey a sense of involved and peaceful care and guidance. Today pastors prone to fire shots in the air may find the sheep scattered and difficult to round up.

PRAYING WITH SCRIPTURE

- Those involved in any form of pastoral ministry might reflect on whether the "pastoral" qualities of the readings shape their lives.

- Read prayerfully all of Psalm 23, which, though used often at funerals, is really a psalm about the journey of life.

Seventeenth Sunday in Ordinary Time

Readings: 2 Kgs 4:42-44; Ps 145:10-11, 15-18; Eph 4:1-6; John 6:1-15

> **"You open your hand / and satisfy the desire of
> every living thing" (Ps 145:16).**

GOOD FOOD AND GREAT LEFTOVERS

This Sunday the Lectionary again abandons Mark, omitting the expected continuation of last Sunday's gospel, where Jesus' compassion leads him to feed the five thousand (Mark 6:35-44), and substituting the Johannine version of the story as an entree to an extended reflection on John's "bread of life" discourse (6:6-69). Though the compilers of the Lectionary may have selected John 6 for five Sunday gospels to provide a chance to enter more deeply into the mystery of the Eucharist, it has become a daunting time for homilists. The chapter is well unified with different motifs subtly interwoven, but the patchwork Lectionary choices do not make sense apart from the larger context. These readings come, at least in the Northern Hemisphere, in the middle of the summer and hardly evoke rapt attention at a sunny, summer Mass. Over the next weeks I will present some reflections on the major themes of the discourse, but with the strong recommendation that the whole chapter be read and reread.

The multiplication of the loaves is the only miracle from Jesus' public ministry narrated in all four Gospels, and in all four has eucharistic overtones. Each has distinctive theological emphases. John locates it specifically at Passover, and Jesus is seated, evoking Moses at Sinai, since the subsequent discourse in John will deal with the manna in the wilderness and use food as a symbol of true teaching. The miracle unfolds quickly. Jesus asks his Philip how they will feed the people. Only John mentions Philip, who later will bring "Greeks" to Jesus, anticipating the inclusions of non-Jews in the Eucharistic banquet. Andrew, Simon's brother, introduces a young man with "five barley loaves and two fishes." In language similar in all four accounts and evocative of the Last Supper, Jesus "took the loaves, gave thanks, and distributed them" to those reclining. John has important distinctive elements: he alone uses the verb *euchariste* ("to give thanks"); Jesus alone distributes the bread and commands the disciples to gather the fragments (using a word that becomes a technical term for eucharistic elements) so that "nothing will be wasted" (literally "perish"), a symbol perhaps of the community to be gathered by Jesus where none may perish (see 3:16; 10:28).

The accounts of the multiplication of the loaves and fishes offer ample material for reflection and prayer. Jesus meets that most basic human need, hunger, with largess and compassion. Meals are a privileged locus to meet Jesus and for the service and gathering of disciples. Yet John uses this story to introduce a profound and extended reflection on the Eucharist and Bread of Life. By placing the action before the long discourse, John indicates that a deeper understanding of the mystery of the Eucharist follows only upon an experience of gracious love.

PRAYING WITH SCRIPTURE

- Jesus is concerned over the hunger of the people. What hungers of the world do you feel trouble Jesus today? How should your community or parish respond?

- The selection from Ephesians has been the charter for the hope of Christian unity. Pray that divided Christians may someday share the same Eucharistic banquet.

Eighteenth Sunday in Ordinary Time

Readings: Exod 16:2-4, 12-15; Ps 78:3-4, 23-25, 54; Eph 4:17, 20-24; John 6:24-35

"For the bread of God is that which comes down from heaven and gives life to the world" (John 6:33).

BREAD ALWAYS FRESH, ALWAYS REFRESHING

One of the characteristics of John's Gospel is that the miracles or "signs" of Jesus serve mainly as occasions for long explanations of the deep meaning of the sign. John plays down both the astonishing character of the miracles and the reactions of the crowds. In its Johannine context the gospel today serves as an introduction to the major themes of the "Bread of Life" discourse and recapitulates major motifs of the Gospel as a whole. The section begins with the familiar Johannine technique of misunderstanding, which also reflects the later rabbinic mode of argument in which a pupil continually poses often incorrect questions to a teacher on the journey to wisdom.

After the multiplication of the loaves the crowds hail Jesus as prophet and want to make him king, so he withdraws from them. When they find him, they ask, "When did you get here [Capernaum]?" The question serves as foil for Jesus to say that they were interested only in the material benefits of the feeding without seeing that it was a symbol of the "food that endures for eternal life" and which the Son of Man will give. Highly condensed in this answer is a summary of the whole ministry of Jesus. He will come to bring eternal life, that is, the fullness of life to people, and this will be brought about through the cross, when the Son of Man who is lifted up will draw all people to himself (John 12:32).

The misunderstanding continues in the next question posed by the crowds, who seek some easy way to perform the works of God (such as the multiplication of loaves). The Johannine Jesus responds with another foundational theme of the Gospel: "This is the work of God, that you believe in the one he sent" (John 6:29). At the conclusion, in John 20:31, the evangelist will comment, "These [things] are written that you may [come to] believe that Jesus is the Messiah, the Son of God, and that through belief you may have life in his name." Believing, which is never a noun in John (that is faith), is the aim of the whole Gospel and challenges readers to accept the extraordinary claim that in the very text of the Gospel they encounter the transcendent God in the person of the Word made flesh.

Yet another misunderstanding is posed to Jesus, where the crowd seems to oppose this "work" with the gift of manna in the desert (a miraculous work of God), which Jesus again counters by saying that the manna was not a miracle of Moses, God's gift of bread from heaven, and that God's bread from heaven gives life to the world, and he is the bread of life, so that "whoever comes to me will never hunger, and whoever believes in me will never thirst" (6:35). The next major section of the discourse extends from this saying to its repetition in 6:51, when in clear eucharistic language Jesus will speak of eating his flesh and drinking his blood.

Two major themes are woven into the tapestry of this discourse which help to shape eucharistic theology today. In the Jewish tradition the manna in the desert came to be associated with the giving of the Torah, so that believers are nurtured by God's teaching as were their ancestors in the wilderness, and the wisdom of God is often portrayed by the metaphor of food. Throughout the first section of the discourse (6:24-51), while speaking of the bread of life, Jesus uses language of believing, drawing near, and listening, terms that are associated more with assimilation of wisdom than eating. The full participation in eating the body and drinking the blood of Jesus (6:55-56) follows upon personal commitment and love which draws a person to absorb the teaching of Jesus and imitate his life given for others (John 13:34; 15:12).

John's Jesus today says that the bread of God which comes down from heaven "gives life to the *world*" and that "whoever comes to me will never hunger, and whoever believes in me will never thirst." Jesus then says, "I will not reject anyone who comes to me." The eucharistic discipline of the Church, especially by not exploring more open eucharist hospitality, is in tension with this Johannine theology. Should people who have been nurtured by the teaching of Jesus be excluded from eucharistic participation? Can Christians be urged to respond fully to John 6:1-51 and be denied the gift of John 6:52-59? Baptized Christians, in the words of the second reading, form a new people "created in God's way in righteousness and holiness of truth" (Eph 4:24). How will they participate in the fullness of this life?

PRAYING WITH SCRIPTURE

- Parents who are guiding their children in the teaching of Jesus should prayerfully reflect that they are nurturing them with "the bread of life."

- Repeat often in prayer that the major "work" God seeks from us is to believe in "the one he has sent."

Nineteenth Sunday in Ordinary Time

Readings: 1 Kgs 19:4-8; Ps 34:2-9; Eph 4:30–5:2; John 6:41-51

**"Be imitators of God, as beloved children,
and live in love, as Christ loved us" (Eph 5:1-2).**

LET'S DO DINNER

The gospel plunges us directly into the middle of the "Bread of Life" discourse, which, despite its seeming complexity, develops two major themes: people will attain eternal life by coming to Jesus and being in union with him; this coming and living in union flow from God's gracious initiative manifest in Jesus. The discourse also has deep roots in biblical tradition.

The discourse takes place in the wilderness, where God first gave miraculous food to people, the manna, which the people ate and then died, in contrast to the living bread of Jesus, which gives eternal life. While the eucharistic reference echoes throughout the discourse and is explicit in next Sunday's gospel, in the Old Testament images of feeding are associated with God's gift of wisdom, so much so that even in patristic times the teaching of Jesus was interpreted as the bread of life, and in the later Jewish tradition manna was interpreted as "teaching."

In John 6:35, for example, Jesus says, "I am the bread of life; whoever comes to me will never hunger, and whoever believes in me will never thirst." This recalls the invitation of Wisdom (Sir 24:19-21) to come to her so that "[those] who eat me will hunger still; [those] who drink me will thirst for more" (24:20; see Sir 15:3). In Proverbs 9:4-6 Wisdom prepares a feast for her devotees and invites them, "Come, eat of my food, / and drink of the wine I have mixed" (Prov 9:5, first reading for next Sunday).

These Old Testament motifs have implications for a rich understanding of the Eucharist today. As bread given in the wilderness, it is food for a pilgrim people, even a rebellious one: "Stop murmuring among yourselves." Most importantly, the presence of Jesus in the Eucharist cannot be separated from the "wisdom" his life communicates. Every reception of the Eucharist must be an act of faith in the teaching of Jesus and a commitment to that life enfleshed in Jesus, to which he invites all who would be followers. The bread that Jesus gives as his "flesh for the life of the world" is what Jesus teaches and embodies, principally the love command (13:34-35; 15:9-15). It is sad that in the contemporary Church many of the most bitter disputes from tabernacle placement to details of celebration style center on the Eucharist. This is not the bread of life.

PRAYING WITH SCRIPTURE

- The word "Amen," said as we receive the body of Christ, comes from the Hebrew root "to believe." Make each Eucharist a renewal of faith.

- Pray about ways in which the teaching of Jesus in John may become wisdom to guide your life.

Twentieth Sunday in Ordinary Time

Readings: Prov 9:1-6; Ps 34:2-7; Eph 5:15-20; John 6:51-58

"Taste and see the goodness of the Lord" (Ps 34:2).

You Are What You Eat

The symphony of the Bread of Life discourse reaches a crescendo with startling hopes and startling claims. "Whoever eats my flesh and drinks my blood has eternal life, and I will raise him on the last day" (6:54). Though we tend to identify "eternal life" as the promised reward following death, in John it begins in this life as a gift from Jesus. Earlier Jesus says: "Amen, amen, I say to you, whoever hears my word and believes in the one who sent me has eternal life and will not come to condemnation, but has passed from death to life" (5:24). Eternal life in John is a present possession that reaches its fulfillment in total "abiding" with God; it is the life of faith, a kind and quality of life that those who follow Jesus lead, but a kind that will not be destroyed by death. People of faith participate in this life while alive. It is the life that is sustained by eating Jesus' flesh and blood.

The utter realism of eating flesh and drinking blood was shocking to Jesus' hearers, as it would be today if taken literally. (Imagine the shocked reaction if a chalice of blood was placed on a table next to a chalice of consecrated wine simply to bring home the "transformation.") Talk of flesh and blood is meant to shock and to bring home the realism of the full humanity of Jesus. John clearly understands these terms symbolically or "sacramentally." The Johannine Jesus is truly a heavenly figure, come from above, returning to the Father possessing present supernatural knowledge, tripping lightly on earth, as commentators have noted. John became with some justification a favorite of later Gnostics, who denied the full humanity of Jesus.

Here the shocking language and startled reaction of the audience serves as a challenge to believers to affirm the seemingly impossible. In receiving the Eucharist, our full humanity is joined with the full but transformed humanity of Jesus, and this constitutes life in its fullness, which will never be taken away. Andre Dubus described this eloquently in *Meditations from a Movable Chair:* "When the priest places the Host in the palm of my hand, I put in my mouth and taste and chew and swallow the intimacy of God."

PRAYING WITH SCRIPTURE

- Pray in gratitude at communion that in being united with the humanity of Jesus, our own humanity becomes the carrier of God's presence.

- Thinking of loved ones who have died, pray quietly Jesus' words, "Whoever eats this bread will live forever."

Twenty-First Sunday in Ordinary Time

Readings: Josh 24:1-2a, 15-17, 18b; Ps 34:2-3, 16-21; Eph 5:21-32;
John 6:60-69

"The words I have spoken to you are Spirit and life" (John 6:63).

CRUNCH TIME

As John 6 comes to an end, the meaning of Jesus' eloquent yet mysterious words sinks in. Many of Jesus' disciples say, "This saying is hard; who can accept it?" The moment of decision has arrived, as it arrived when Joshua summoned "all the tribes of Israel" to renew the covenant. In an in-your-face address, Joshua says, "If it does not please you to serve the LORD, decide today whom you will serve," foreign gods or "the Lord." The people renew their devotion to the Lord, "who brought us and our fathers up out of the land of Egypt, out of a state of slavery." Recollection of the life-giving power of God leads to commitment.

Faced with shock and doubt, Jesus says that the words he has spoken are given by the Son of Man ("the human one"), who will return to God's presence—that is, they possess divine authority. Somewhat enigmatically, having just urged people to eat his flesh, he says, "It is the spirit that gives life, while the flesh is of no avail" (John 6:63) and that his words are "Spirit and life." John plays here on the double meaning of flesh, using it here in a negative sense as a way of viewing the world influenced by human expectations and human prejudices. Spirit is openness to God's revelation and in that sense "gives life," just as God's creative Spirit gave life to the world and inspired Moses and the prophets.

Many of Jesus' disciples return "to their former way of life," and he turns to the Twelve and asks if they want to leave. Beyond problems with church teaching and practice, beyond active engagement in social concern and even personal struggles, there is Jesus present saying, "Do you also want to leave?" This is acutely symbolic of the choices facing people on their religious journey. Even the most profound revelation of Jesus, that he is God's wisdom for humanity and that all who eat his flesh and drink his blood will have fullness of life, does not take away the mystery of human freedom. God's gifts are extraordinary and inviting, but when faced with them, people can return to their former life. Amid often conflicting claims about what it means to be a Catholic today, we must hear Peter's words to Jesus resounding through the centuries: "To whom shall we go? You have the words of eternal life."

PRAYING WITH SCRIPTURE

- Read again John 6, reflecting on how these "words" of Jesus are Spirit and life.

- The one who believes already possesses "eternal life." Think in prayer about how faith leads us to a fullness of life.

- Ask in prayer with Peter, "To whom shall we go?"

Twenty-Second Sunday in Ordinary Time

Readings: Deut 4:1-2, 6-8; Ps 15:2-5; Jas 1:17-18, 21b-22, 27;
Mark 7:1-8; 14-15, 21-23

"Be doers of the word, and not hearers only" (Jas 1:22).

Look into Your Hearts!

Having completed a long tour through John 6, the Lectionary returns to Mark with a dispute between Jesus, the Pharisees, and some scribes (experts in the law) over rules to assure purity when eating. The readings present something of a paradox. The first reading, the beginning of the prayer that Jews are to recite every day (the Shema, "Hear, O Israel") heralds the beauty of the law given to Israel and its observance as a sign of gratitude for the promise of the land.

The responsorial psalm describes a person who lives justly before God, and James summons people to care for the widow and the orphan, a frequent motif in Israel's law. Yet in the gospel Jesus criticizes Pharisaic observance and says that interior dispositions alone determine true purity.

The gospel presents a constant danger of contrasting Christianity as a religion of love and interior conversion to "legalistic" Judaism. What it recounts is clearly an inner-Jewish dispute. The Pharisees were primarily a lay group dedicated to strict observance of the Temple regulations for purity in their daily lives as a sign that every aspect of life could be holy. They developed a series of traditions "to build a fence around the Law," so that the Law itself would never be violated. In response Jesus stands in the prophetic tradition by citing Isaiah 29:13, where the prophet castigates the tendency to "disregard God's commandment but cling to human tradition."

Tradition is essential not only to human life but to all religion as the narratives, rituals, and beliefs of a community are handed on and adapted to new situations. But the gospel warns against the tendency inherent in every religion to equate traditional "human precepts" with God's will. The Jewish-Christian letter of James, the second reading for the next five Sundays, captures the spirit of traditional Jewish piety, in which love of God is to be translated into deeds of loving kindness toward the vulnerable members of the community. Against this there is no law.

In the gospel Jesus speaks not to the Pharisees and scribes, but to his disciples, warning them of those evils that can pollute the human heart and destroy social relationships. Though these sound a bit like the coming episodes of television talk shows presided over by various Jerrys and Jennys, they remain a frightening warning to would-be followers of Jesus. As summer vacations draw to an end, preachers might use these readings to challenge people to renewal by examining those traditional ways of acting and thinking that reflect "mere human precepts" instead of God's will, and summon them to look into their own hearts, making perhaps a list of those destructive attitudes that can infect even the hearts of those closest to Jesus.

PRAYING WITH SCRIPTURE

- James calls God "the Father of lights." Recall in prayer times when God's word has been a light to your path.

- Pray about ways in which set habits of acting (human traditions) can lead our hearts away from God (Isa 29:13).

Twenty-Third Sunday in Ordinary Time

Readings: Isa 35:4-7a; Ps 146:7-10; Jas 2:1-5; Mark 7:31-37

**"The God of Jacob keeps faith forever;
secures justice for the oppressed" (Ps 146:7).**

A PARTIAL GOD

While last Sunday's readings sounded sober warnings, today's readings celebrate the saving deeds of God. The reading from Isaiah opens with one of the most frequent biblical commands, "Fear not," and then looks to the divine deliverance from exile when the blind, deaf, lame, and speechless will be healed and praise God. The psalm sings of a God who gives sight to the blind, raises up those who are bowed down, and welcomes strangers, a theme that is then picked up in James. The gospel is a virtual fulfillment of Isaiah, as Jesus heals a deaf man who is unable to speak.

While both Isaiah and the gospel long for physical healing, the ailments listed are also symbolic of interior sufferings, consisting often of blindness to the needs of the neighbor, inability to hear God's voice and move beyond a certain place, or to speak words of praise and consolation. James captures this with vivid irony when the people welcome the person fashionably dressed with gold rings while ignoring the poor man, who is poor only in the eyes of the world but is rich in faith.

These readings pose a special challenge today as prosperity seems to grow by leaps and bounds, along with blindness toward those left aside by the "new economy" or who cannot even "speak plainly" about their concerns.

Yet the readings speak of a God who is partial to the voiceless and afflicted. Jesus enters the world of the speechless with healing touches and gestures. The person healed becomes a witness to the power of God. A Church that is to witness to its Jewish heritage and to the example of Jesus must be partial to "those who were bowed down" and through its healing presence give a voice to the voiceless.

PRAYING WITH SCRIPTURE

- Isaiah proclaims to frightened hearts, "Be strong, fear not." Ask for the strength to "speak plainly" of God's saving deeds.

- Reading the gospel again, pray for someone you know who suffers from hearing and speech problems, and think how you might better understand him or her.

September 14

The Exaltation of the Holy Cross

Readings: Num 21:4b-9; Ps 78:1-2, 34-38; Phil 2:6-11; John 3:13-17

**"For God so loved the world that he gave his
only Son" (John 3:16).**

BEHOLD THE WOOD OF THE CROSS!

What an extraordinary scene etched on the wall of a second-century Roman building like some graffiti at a big-city underpass! A line-drawn figure stares up at a crucified donkey, with the rough inscription, "Alexamenos adores his God." Before crosses adorned our churches and glimmered on jewelry counters, the cross was a symbol of disgrace and mockery. Prior to Constantine and the finding of relics of the true cross (A.D. 326), there is little evidence of the cross in primitive Christian art.

Yet one of the most fundamental and pervasive theological motifs in the New Testament is the celebration of God's love manifest in the cross as a shorthand way of proclaiming the suffering, death, and resurrection of Jesus. Crucifixes have portrayed Jesus as a royal figure reigning from the cross (Byzantine art) and as an anguished figure covered with plague sores (the medieval *Pestkreuze*). The chapel at Xavier castle in Navarre contains an extraordinary crucifix dating back before the time of St. Francis Xavier. The cross is surrounded by the images of the dance of death, but on the face of the Christ figure is an iconic smile, symbolizing the ultimate irony that as death dances, death is defeated by the suffering of the author of life.

The "Christ Hymn" from Philippians is one of the earliest confessions of faith, perhaps used at baptism. It portrays Jesus as one who, though equal to God, did not consider this something to be grasped (or held on to tightly) but emptied himself. Unlike Adam, who was tempted to be like God (Gen 3:4), Jesus comes "in human likeness" and suffers not just Adam's fate, death, but the horrible death on a cross.

110

Here the hymn turns with a resounding "therefore" (RSV), as God exalts Jesus and sets him up as Lord of the universe. Paul cites this hymn to urge his community, not toward martyrdom, but to have the mind of Christ by considering others as more important than themselves and to practice communal love. The cross touches everyday life.

The gospel begins with one of the most enigmatic statements in the New Testament and ends with one of the most quoted sayings of Jesus (3:16-17). In the middle of a long conversation with Nicodemus, alluding to his crucifixion, Jesus says that the Son of Man must be lifted up (John's allusion to the crucifixion/exaltation of Jesus), so that everyone who believes in him will have eternal life. The shocking thing is the comparison with the lifting up of Jesus and Moses lifting up that ancient symbol of evil, the serpent, in the desert. The account in Numbers 21 is one of the many occasions when the liberated people begin to murmur against Moses. This time it is a complaint over the "wretched food." The Lord reacts quickly and harshly; snakes infest the people, biting them, and many die. Having experienced God's judgment, they cry to Moses, "We have sinned in complaining against the LORD and you. Pray the LORD to take the serpents from us." The Lord instructs Moses to make a bronze serpent and to raise it on high, and anyone who looks on it will be healed.

The allusion takes on a totally new meaning in John. Jesus is the one who is lifted as the saving figure, but not as a remedy for God's harsh judgment, but because "God so loved the world that he gave his only Son, so that everyone who believes in him might not perish but might have eternal life." In his intriguing and original comments, Jack Miles notes "how hauntingly the next lines resound against the now awakened memory of God's revenge, as God protests *this* time that he has not come to judge but that 'through him [his Son] the world might be saved'" (*Christ: A Crisis in the Life of God* [Alfred A. Knopf, 2001] 50–51).

To celebrate the Triumph of the Cross is to celebrate a litany of deep mysteries and paradoxes. Through death, death is conquered; a new creation begins as the Incarnate Creator dies. Eternal life, that is, life in its fullness, arises from gazing on a figure of death. This profound mystery is expressed in things as seemingly jejune as considering others better than one's self and walking united in minds and hearts (Phil 2:1-5). Are Christian lives today any less puzzling to the world around than that of Alexamenos?

PRAYING WITH SCRIPTURE

- Holding a crucifix, pray quietly, repeating John 3:16-17.

- Pray in gratitude for those who are examples of the profound mystery of the defeat of death and suffering through their own suffering.

- As St. Paul states, the example of Jesus should touch ordinary life. Pray over areas where having the mind of Christ can bring healing from division and strife.

Twenty-Fifth Sunday in Ordinary Time

Readings: Wis 2:12, 17-20; Ps 54:3-5, 6-8; Jas 3:16–4:3; Mark 9:30-37

"I will walk before the LORD, / in the land of the living" (Ps 116:9).

CAN YOU WALK THE WALK?

Christians today tend to think of the age of martyrs in terms of the early centuries of the Church, with vivid pictures of lions about to devour those who would not deny Christ. Yet Karl Rahner once noted that today we should speak not only of martyrs of the faith but also of martyrs of justice. The readings today bring home that such martyrs are deeply rooted in the Bible.

The first reading provides the best example of the motif of the just person who suffers, yet is vindicated by God. The just person by his or her very life stands against those who have lost a sense of God and pursue only "the good things that are real" (Wis 2:6) and make their "strength the norm of justice" (2:11).

The gospel contains Jesus' teaching on the "way" of discipleship as he makes his "way" toward his death. A dramatic characteristic of this section is that the chosen disciples consistently misunderstand his teaching, preferring to talk rather about questions of prestige and rank in the community (see esp. Mark 10:32-45, the gospel for the Twenty-Ninth Sunday in Ordinary Time, Cycle B).

In today's gospel, after having witnessed the dramatic miracle of the healing of the epileptic boy (9:14-29), where they were unable to cast out the spirit causing the illness, and after hearing Jesus teaching on faith and prayer, the disciples hear again Jesus' prediction of suffering and death. The disciples again are not sure what Jesus means, and when he asks them what they were discussing, they cannot answer. But Mark tells us that they "had been discussing among themselves on the way who was the greatest." The irony here is profound. "On the way," when they should have been reflecting on the mystery of their call to follow Jesus and bear the cross, they trade ambitious desires. Jesus then calls "the Twelve," the symbol of the reconstituted people who are to embody his values, places a child right in front of them, and says that whoever receives "one child such as this in my name, receives me."

To understand the power of Jesus' prophetic and symbolic action, we should not think of children simply as loving and innocent. At the time of Jesus children were "non-persons," without any power and often unprotected, and they function as symbols of powerlessness and vulnerability. Contrary to the disciples' desire for positions of power in God's kingdom, Jesus says they should be more concerned with welcoming into their midst the poor and vulnerable and by so doing receive both Jesus and the One who sent him (cf. Matt 25:31-46).

Today just people will be rejected, persecuted, and even killed for things as apolitical as directing a school or feeding the hungry, since these can be affronts to the lifestyle of the powerful. I recall a former Jesuit student from the Jesuit School of Theology at Berkeley, Andre Masse, who worked at St. Joseph's College in Tyre, Lebanon. His goal was to provide quality education to both Christian and Muslim youth as a way to break down barriers. One afternoon as the school was closing, two hooded gunmen came into his office and murdered him. He was doing nothing more than providing children an alternative to violence and welcoming them.

The gospel reminds the Church today of the dangers of ambition and posturing for positions of power. In recent years the genie of ecclesiastical ambition has been again let out of the bottle, so much so that Cardinal Gantin, dean of the College of Cardinals and former Prefect of the Congregation for Bishops, deplored episcopal careerism and said he was shocked by bishops seeking promotion from smaller to larger dioceses, a view echoed two months later by Cardinal Ratzinger. (Lest I suffer from seeing the speck in another's eye and not the log in my own, the world of academic theology where I live is rife with ambition and self-promotion.) Yet the pilgrim Church of God's people continues the work of justice, and the unprotected and vulnerable are welcomed and protected. Jesus has many unnamed companions today as he follows the path of self-giving for others that leads through death to resurrection.

PRAYING WITH SCRIPTURE

• Read prayerfully Chapter 2 of the book of Wisdom and think of people today who remind you of the suffering just One.

- Pray about ways in which the Church may better welcome "children" into our midst.

- Pray about ways the desire to be "the greatest" shapes life in the United States and how Gospel values can counter it.

Twenty-Sixth Sunday in Ordinary Time

Readings: Num 11:25-29; Ps 19:8, 10, 12-14; Jas 5:1-6; Mark 9:38-43, 45, 47-48

"Would that all the people of the LORD were prophets!"
(Num 11:29).

A CUP OF WATER OR UNQUENCHABLE FIRE

In today's gospel the "sweet Jesus" of much of Christian piety seems to be having a bad day. He rebuffs a disciple, and his sayings echo with images of intentional drowning, self-mutilation, and permanent residence in Gehenna with unquenchable fire. These sayings, which once may have been independent, are linked by key words: name, scandal, life, fire, and are set by Mark in the story of Jesus' journey to Jerusalem, where he teaches about the radical "cost of discipleship."

The gospel begins with a question from John about how to silence someone who was casting out demons in the name of Jesus though he was not a follower. Since Jesus' disciples have just failed to cast out a demon, their desire to be proprietors of God's power rings hollow, especially in light of their previous failure to cast out a "mute spirit" (Mark 9:18). Jesus counters John's view with the saying, "Do not prevent him. . . . Anyone who gives you a cup of water to drink because you belong to Christ, . . . will surely not lose his reward," since "whoever is not against us is for us."

The first reading has been chosen as an Old Testament prefiguration of Jesus' words and actions. Moses has descended from Sinai, and God's spirit descends on the seventy elders and they begin to prophesy. Two are absent, Eldad and Medad, and yet the spirit rests on them and they prophesy. Like John, Joshua asks Moses to stop them, and Moses answers with the hope that God's spirit of prophecy be given to all the people. One motif, then, that characterizes these two readings is that the power and spirit of God cannot be appropriated by any group, even a group of chosen leaders, and that the work of God can be done by someone who was not one of us.

The mood of Jesus' teaching now changes. The setting returns to that of Mark 9:36, where Jesus is holding a child, and now he warns dramatically against causing a little one to sin. "Cause to sin," which puts the onus of sinning on "the little one," is not the best translation of the Greek (lit. "scandalize"), which means rather "cause to fall" or "put an obstacle in a person's way." In the Babylonian Talmud, scandalizing is interpreted as "child abuse." Mark adds four harsh and somewhat exaggerated images that reinforce the consequences of such "scandal" and depict the kind of radical actions one should take rather than harm the little ones and end up in Gehenna.

The readings today, like so much of Mark, present the good news and the sober news. The good news is that those who do the work of Jesus, even without being his followers, are "for him," and that whoever gives even a cup of water in Jesus' name will not lose his or her reward. Today in our parishes people are not simply giving a cup of water but are feeding the hungry and welcoming the stranger, because they too "belong to Christ." Jesus' words here are also a reminder that we must read the signs of the times and discern those outside our communities of disciples who are still confronting the power of evil and are "for us." Moses' action is a warning against domesticating or institutionalizing the voice of prophecy.

The "sober" but paradoxically good news is the sad consequences of causing the little ones to fall, whether they be actual children or vulnerable members of the community. The picture of Jesus holding a child and defending the little ones is especially pertinent in our times. Recently the lead article in the *New York Times Magazine* was "The Backlash Against Children," detailing how highly prosperous people in our society not only resent the physical presence of children but also begrudge the benefits given to families with children. (A long meditation on the second reading from James might be in order, e.g., "You have lived on earth in luxury and pleasure; you have fattened your hearts for the day of slaughter.") Among the twenty-one most affluent nations, the United States has the highest percentage of poor children (almost 25 percent). During this political season, while education and health care are clubs with which both parties batter the other, millions of children sit in poor schools and suffer poor health. Some TV spots on millstones might be a welcome change.

PRAYING WITH SCRIPTURE

- Pray about the ways in which people who are "not of us" can be "for us" and how we often try to prevent them.

- Spend time with the image of Jesus holding the child and pray in gratitude for the gift of children and in sorrow over their neglect.

- Pray about ways in which the voice of prophecy can be heard in the Church today.

Twenty-Seventh Sunday in Ordinary Time

Readings: Gen 2:18-24; Ps 128:1-6; Heb 2:9-11; Mark 10:2-16

> **"Blessed are you who fear the LORD,**
> **who walk in his ways!" (Ps 128:1).**

MARRIAGES ARE MADE IN HEAVEN

Marriage is increasingly described as a fragile institution in our society. Divorce rates hover around 40 percent, with the divorce rate among Catholics at roughly 20 percent. The readings for this Sunday provide a biblical countervision.

The gospel begins with the Pharisees testing Jesus by asking whether it is lawful for a husband to divorce (lit. "send away") his wife. Jesus responds by asking them about the Law, and they quote Deuteronomy 4:1, which allows a husband to divorce his wife by simply writing a bill of divorce (see Matt 1:19). Jesus responds by quoting two sayings from the two creation accounts of Genesis: "male and female he created them" (Gen 1:27), and "the two of them become one flesh" (in today's first reading). Though on paper Jewish first-century divorce legislation seemed to favor "easy divorce," in practice divorce was very infrequent.

Jesus' teaching is not so much an attack on a widespread abuse as it is a prophetic challenge that draws on God's creative purpose. The Genesis texts attribute two essential qualities to marriage: unity (the two shall become one) and complementarity or mutual interdependence. Neither man alone nor woman alone embodies the fullness of God's creative design, but man and woman in union mirror the mystery of God. By negating an interpretation of Deut 24:1-6 that allowed easy divorce, Jesus says in effect that where such a possibility of injustice and inequality exists in marriage, there can be no true marriage according to the intent of Genesis. Jesus views marriage, in which man and woman are no longer two but one, living in unity and interdependence, as a symbol of restored creation. Jesus also utters here a prophetic defense of the innocent victim of divorce, the woman.

119

All the Gospels both hand on and adapt the teaching of Jesus. Mark is aware of the right of the woman to divorce that was allowed in the Roman Empire. While Mark's Gospel hands on an absolute rejection of divorce, in both Matthew (5:32 and 19:9) and Paul (1 Cor 7:12-16) there are stated exceptions. The teaching of Jesus left the Church with a twofold legacy. On the one hand, the Church continues to reiterate Jesus' prophetic defense of marriage. This is done not simply by opposing cultural trends but positively through the evolution of excellent marriage preparation programs involving married couples who speak honestly about the challenges to growth in unity and love. On the other hand, the Church, especially in its revised annulment procedures, recognizes exceptions to an absolute prohibition. The Church must also constantly reflect the pastoral concern of Jesus for those who have suffered divorce. While Jesus presents a vision of what marriage should be, he utters no word of condemnation of "the divorced," and the Gospel of John shows Jesus defending a woman about to be stoned for adultery (7:53–8:11) and giving a special mission to an often-married woman, the Samaritan woman at the well.

Mark appends to Jesus' teaching on marriage another story about Jesus holding a child. Strangely, since they had just heard praises of marriage, the disciples "rebuke" people for bringing the children. While earlier in Mark Jesus said that whoever receives a child receives him, here he says that "the kingdom of God belongs to such as these" and that "whoever does not accept the kingdom of God like a child will not enter it." After proclaiming an ethic of radical discipleship through unity and mutuality in marriage, Jesus is here not praising "childishness" but using the child as a symbol of both non-domination and the need for care that should characterize human relationships. Especially powerful are the final two verses, which describe Jesus, the unmarried prophet, taking the children in his arms and blessing them, an enduring image that should haunt the Christian conscience as we see the horrors of malnourished and disease-ridden children both at home and abroad.

Praying with Scripture

- Married people might pray in gratitude about how their lives have been images of the creative love of God.

- Spend some time praying for people about to be married and for married friends facing special challenges.

- Pray about ways that local parish communities might become stronger advocates for children.

Twenty-Eighth Sunday in Ordinary Time

Readings: Wis 7:7-11; Ps 90:12-17; Heb 4:12-13; Mark 10:17-30

**"The word of God is living and effective,
sharper than any two-edged sword" (Heb 4:12).**

DON'T GO AWAY SAD!

The classical music station paused for an ad. A couple about to be wed were visiting a marriage counselor. They were having their first "fight"—over what kind of SUV to buy. He wanted a Mercedes, but she had heard that the Mercedes was a big, lumbering car. Then he explained that the new Mercedes was wonderful, sleek, easy to handle, and cost only $35,000! Premarital bliss was restored, and the marriage counselor gushed lovingly over the reconciliation. Such are the values marketed to the new elite in the "new economy."

The challenge posed by wealth is as old as the Hebrew prophets and formed a vital part of Jesus' teaching. In today's gospel "a young man ran up," clearly eager to obtain eternal life. He called Jesus "Good teacher," and Jesus responded with a put-down, "No one is good but God alone." Jesus then challenged the young man by listing those precepts of the Decalogue that deal with social and familial relations. Having learned his lesson, the young man now simply addressed Jesus as "Teacher" and stated that he had observed all these from his youth. Jesus looked on him, loved him, and challenged him to sell what he had, give the money to the poor, and then follow him. Jesus' disciples were to travel light (Mark 6:7-9) and to imitate the powerlessness of the child (10:13-15). His enthusiasm crushed, the young man went away sad, "for he had many possessions," and Jesus said (harshly or sadly, we don't know),"How hard it is for those who have wealth to enter the kingdom of God."

The story then switches. The disciples, who themselves sought power and prestige (Mark 9:34; 10:37), were amazed, since riches can be a sign of God's favor. But Jesus now intensified the difficulty with the some-

121

what ludicrous and exaggerated image of a camel trying to go through the eye of a needle. There is also irony here: "many possessions" are carried on camels. Now dumbfounded, they asked, "Who can be saved?" Without really answering, Jesus simply said that what we think is impossible is possible with God.

The real thrust of today's gospel comes when Peter, the usual foil in Mark for misunderstanding, said, in effect, "We have left everything, but what's in it for us?" For all followers of Jesus, the answer was as challenging as it was for the rich man. What you get are new houses, new lands, new brothers and sisters, a hundred times more in this life, but "with persecutions" and eternal life (which the young man was seeking).

Though vivid and powerful, this gospel is also as puzzling and shocking for contemporary Christians as it was for Jesus' first disciples. Radical divesting of wealth hardly characterizes Church life (and Church leaders), so Jesus' teaching is interpreted frequently as an evangelical counsel for a few, though Jesus speaks of the difficulty of salvation "for those having wealth"—that is, "all" of them. The Church also depends on the generosity of people of means for ordinary parish life and social outreach. Yet there are important hints about how this gospel may speak to people today.

Strangely, Jesus loves the young man (embodying his own love for the Law and the Prophets), yet later says that it will be difficult for him to enter God's kingdom. Though the youth was observant of commands, he did not realize that the love of Jesus was leading him beyond his virtue. Often Christ challenges people to a more intense discipleship, not at their point of weakness, but precisely at their point of strength. Acquired virtue and dutifulness must yield to an uncertain future. Yet the future is not bleak, since Jesus promises a "hundredfold" in this life. The list includes lands, new families, even amid persecution.

These joys reflect the experience of the early Church, with its new sense of community and new familial relationships. Hospitality, reception of traveling missionaries, care for the poor, and mutual love (new houses, new lands, new families) were hallmarks of early Christianity ("See how they love one another," said the pagans).

There are far deeper values and far deeper joys than great possessions can assure. Dorothy Day once said that the important thing about the *Catholic Worker* was not poverty but community, and in her wonderful reminiscences, *On Pilgrimage,* she tells of getting off a Greyhound bus in a city, not knowing exactly where she would stay, but finding houses, brothers and sisters (and often opposition or arrest). Perhaps the Church today should seek ways to go by Greyhound rather than by SUV.

PRAYING WITH SCRIPTURE

- Imagine yourself in the place of the young man; think of what Jesus would love in you.

- Pray about ways that our culture can distort our values in regard to "many possessions."

- Pray in gratitude for those experiences of new brothers and sisters, new homes and new lands that have been yours in the family of the Church.

Twenty-Ninth Sunday in Ordinary Time

Readings: Isa 53:10-11; Ps 33:4-5, 18-19, 20, 22; Heb 4:14-16;
Mark 10:35-45

"But it shall not be so among you" (Mark 10:43).

WHAT, ME BECOME A SLAVE!

Often the good "news" of Jesus Christ is turned into good "advice" when the emphasis is placed on what we should do rather than on what God has done for us. Today's readings resound with exclamations of the saving love of God. Isaiah heralds the servant who through his suffering will justify many, which the Church applies to Jesus. The letter to the Hebrews speaks of a high priest who is able to sympathize with us in our weakness because he has been tested in every way, though sinless, and so we can "confidently" hope for God's mercy. The psalm sings beautifully that "of the kindness of the LORD the earth is full." The gospel reading (the longer form is preferable) concludes the Markan journey to Jerusalem, during which Jesus repeatedly spoke of his imminent suffering, only to be misunderstood by his disciples. This rhythm culminates in the desire of James and John for positions of power and the jealousy of the Twelve, which is countered by Jesus' own adoption of the role of Isaiah's servant as the Son of Man, who gives his life as a ransom for many. Today's readings are Christmas in advance as we celebrate gifts almost too startling to believe.

I remember vividly my ordination retreat in May 1964. The director began every reflection with Mark 10:45: "The Son of Man came not to be served but to serve and to give his life as a ransom for many." He stressed constantly that our priesthood was to be a priesthood of service in a servant Church. The service was not simply to be available but a service that brought liberation to people. In the time of Jesus ransom was the price paid to free someone from slavery; sometimes the ransomer offered himself as a substitute for the slave. Jesus' offering was to be a liberating offering. In almost thirty-seven years as a priest I have come to see again and again that this liberating service plays out in the lives of priests but is also constantly realized in the myriad forms of service by the priestly people of God, "for Christ plays in ten thousand places, / Lovely in limbs, and lovely in eyes not his" (Gerard Manley Hopkins).

While the good news may not be good advice, the gracious acts of God call for a response of gratitude and loving service. Mark states this but also offers a countervision embodied in the ambitious and squabbling disciples. After Jesus' most explicit prediction of his suffering, James and John skip the thought of suffering and ask to be vice-regents with Jesus when he comes into his glory. Jesus answers that they may not receive this request, but they will follow his way of suffering. Missing the point as usual, the other disciples become riled up, and Jesus gives them a lesson on what power means in his community.

Gentile rulers lord over their subjects, and their great ones make their authority felt (throw their weight around). "But it shall not be so among you," responds Jesus, a sentence that should be emblazoned on every letter of appointment to a position of authority in the Church. Rather, greatness in Jesus' community is a greatness of service. Gentile, that is Roman, power was exercised primarily through force, intimidation, and an elaborate network of patronage that tried to assure absolute loyalty to the emperor. The way power is maintained in the secular world of rulers and ruled is anathema to true followers of Jesus.

Scripture is both a beautiful tapestry of God's loving deeds and a mirror that enables us to gaze at our own lives. Today's liturgical readings, especially the gospel, console us with a love of God that makes issues of power and dominance irrelevant. Yet they also warn the Church against the misuse of power. "Lording it over" and use of "the heavy hand of authority" are not to characterize the community of disciples. The slavery mandated by Jesus is a loving service of liberation for others. It shines forth in parents at the bed of a sick child, in a spouse caring for another with Alzheimer's disease, in people giving their lives to protest injustice, and in priests and pastoral teams serving local churches. This service draws on a deeper source of power epitomized in St. Paul's statement, "I will gladly glory in my weakness that the power of Christ may dwell in me" (2 Cor 12:9, au. trans.).

PRAYING WITH SCRIPTURE

- Pray about the readings, dwelling on a phrase or two that are "good news" in your life.

- Prayerfully recollect times when your service to others has brought freedom to them—and you.

- Pray that the Church in all its ministries may reflect not the way of the "Gentiles" but the way of the Son of Man.

Thirtieth Sunday in Ordinary Time

Readings: Jer 31:7-9; Ps 126:1-6; Heb 5:1-6; Mark 10:46-52

"Take courage; get up, Jesus is calling you" (Mark 10:49).

SEEING THE LIGHT

The gospel concludes the journey of Jesus to Jerusalem that was inaugurated by the healing of a blind man (8:22-26), which symbolizes the journey of discipleship for followers of Jesus. It also provides a contrast to the failure of the disciples throughout the journey and presents a mini-drama of the path to faith. The narrative erupts with action. The blind man sits begging; he hears and cries out with a cry for saving help, "Jesus, son of David, have pity on me." Many, most likely the followers of Jesus from Mark 10:46, rebuke him, but Jesus "stops" and simply says, "Call him." Others speak out and tell the blind man, "Take courage. . . . Jesus is calling you." Bartimaeus then throws off his cloak, jumps up and comes to Jesus. In response to Jesus' simple question, "What do you want me to do for you?" he says, "Master, I want to see." Echoing his earlier response to the suffering woman (5:34), Jesus says, "Go your way; your faith has saved you." But the man does not go his way; he follows "on the way" with Jesus.

Bartimaeus is one of those "little people" of faith in Mark who embody true discipleship in contrast to the blundering disciples. The narrative may also reflect stages in the journey of faith of many in Mark's community. A person is in dire need, blind and begging; he or she hears of Jesus, utters a prayer for help, meets strong opposition, but persists in prayer ("kept calling"); others in the community help the person and speak of the call of Jesus. Bartimaeus throws aside his cloak (symbolizing perhaps the baptismal divesting). A meeting with Jesus brings the gift of sight, and the person becomes a disciple.

This gospel could be an acted parable of journeys to faith for many people who are being initiated into the Church as adults. The Rite of

Christian Initiation of Adults and other programs that help nominal or lapsed Catholics to return are among the most vital movements in the Church today. These are Scripture-based, as people "hear" of Jesus, and generally are lay directed. Millions of people at different stages of life sit by some road, not able to see where they are going. Through friends or by other promptings of God's Spirit, they hear of Jesus; opposition often follows. Still others enter their isolated world with encouragement ("take courage"); they throw off many old garments, come directly to Christ, and hear his saving voice saying simply that their faith, that is, their loving trust and hope in the face of opposition, will make them whole (save them). They become disciples in a community of disciples. These programs of entrance and return not only witness to the conversion of people to a deep understanding of God's mercy and love, they also convert the converters, who as companions on the journey find their own faith revitalized.

Praying with Scripture

- In moments when you cannot see the way ahead, place yourself with Bartimaeus and ask for Christ's saving help.

- Pray over the second reading from Hebrews thinking of Jesus as the priest who deals patiently with the "ignorant and the erring."

Commemoration of All the Faithful Departed (All Souls)

Readings: Wis 4:7-14; Ps. 25:6, 7b, 17-18, 20-21; 1 Cor 15:51-57; John 11:17-27

> **"Where, O death is your victory?"**
> **"Where, O death is your sting?"**
> **(1 Cor 15:53-54; Hos 13:14).**

LIFE AT DEATH'S DOOR

Commemoration of the faithful departed has a long history in the Church. St. Augustine speaks of his mother celebrating meals at the tombs of the dead, and in early Christian art the names of departed loved ones were entered on diptychs. By the early Middle Ages such commemoration had spread throughout the Western Church. Since the Second Vatican Council, the feast has undergone a transformation from a somber prayer for the departed, with concern for their expiatory sufferings in purgatory, to a celebration of the victory over death through the saving event of Christ.

As reassuring as are the New Testament resurrection texts and the power of the liturgy, death brings in its wake sadness and sorrow, and confronts us with a future known only through faith. Today's gospel, which is the centerpiece of the longer account of the raising of Lazarus, offers a narrative theology of the Christian mystery of life and death.

The story begins simply with a message brought to Jesus from Martha and Mary that "the one you love is ill." As an overture to the whole narrative, Jesus says that "this illness is not to end in death, but is for the glory of God," followed by the Evangelist's comment that "Jesus loved Martha and her sister and Lazarus." Surprisingly, Jesus delays two days and arrives where today's gospel picks up, which becomes

"Martha's story." Expressing her faith in Jesus, she says that "whatever you ask of God, God will give you." Jesus responds simply, "Your brother will rise."

Following the familiar Johannine technique of misunderstanding, Martha affirms her faith in the general resurrection. Jesus says no more for the moment about Lazarus and utters those words that bring so much hope during a funeral liturgy, "I am the resurrection and life; he [she] who believes in me, even if he [she] dies, will live." Martha then affirms that Jesus is the Messiah and Son of God who is coming into the world—that same confession uttered by Peter in the Gospel of Matthew (16:16).

Though today's gospel concludes here, the denouement of the narrative is crucial. Jesus arrives at the village and meets Mary at the tomb. Seeing her weeping, Jesus becomes "perturbed and deeply troubled." Arriving at the tomb, "Jesus wept." The realism of the narrative here underscores John's theology that the Word truly became flesh. Like every human being, Jesus feels the loss of one he loved and mourns in the face of death. Yet he comes to the tomb and orders the stone rolled back. Enhancing the realism, Martha protests that Lazarus has been dead four days, and "there will be a stench," (a bit less vivid than the older translations, "Lord, he stinketh"). Jesus then shouts "Lazarus, come out!" And Lazarus emerges still wrapped in the burial clothes, symbolizing that he will still die again, unlike Jesus, who leaves the wrappings of death in the tomb.

This engaging story conceals a profound theology. Jesus listens to the prayers of those who love him, but in ways and at times of his choosing. Even death is to give glory to God. Martha is a symbol of one who, even in the face of death and a seemingly unanswered prayer, can make the most profound confession of faith. The mystery of the Incarnation is luminous. Jesus is the one who grants eternal (that is, authentic) life, which can never be taken away; he is Messiah and Son of God, yet when seeing the suffering of one he loved (Mary) and standing at death's door, he weeps. Lazarus emerging is a symbol that death can not lock in its dark chambers those whom Jesus loves.

And yet death remains a mystery that causes apprehension and fear in the holiest of people. What comes next? As more naïve images of heaven fade, what follows? Throughout 1 Corinthians 15 Paul wrestled with this question, "How are the dead raised?" Paul does not speak of immortal souls but of resurrection of the body, using the image of new life coming from a seed that corrupts in the ground, and he affirms that what is raised is a "spiritual body." Christian faith is not in immortality of a soul but in resurrection of the body. In Paul the body is not simply flesh and blood, but rather that which gives continuity to life through history and which allows humans to relate to other people. Body is the presupposition for community.

Through faith we all trust that some day we will be remembered as "faithfully departed." Such is our belief in "eternal life" and the resurrection of the body. Our history will be part of our glory, and those people with whom our bodies linked us in this life will be part of our communion in God. Yet this remains a mystery. On feasts like today we naturally recall departed loved ones, especially those who gave us our earthly body. My mother died fourteen years ago at age eighty-nine of a brain tumor. Since she was cared for at home with great love by my sister and by Hospice, we spent many graced hours with her during her last months. One day she and I were talking about "what comes next." I said, "Mom, are you frightened?" A woman of great faith, she said, "No, but I am mighty curious!" I think learned theologians call that belief in the face of mystery.

PRAYING WITH SCRIPTURE

- Bring to prayer those departed who have been especially close to you during the past year.

- Read prayerfully John 11, allowing grief and sorrow of lost loved ones to surface as you hear Jesus' words of promise.

- Memorize and repeat prayerfully John 11:25: "I am the resurrection and life. Those who have faith in me, even though they die, will live" (au. trans.).

November 9

The Dedication of the Lateran Basilica

Readings: Ezek 47:1-2, 8-9, 12; Ps. 46:2-3, 5-6, 8-9; 1 Cor 3:9c-11,
16-17; John 2:13-22

**"Do you not know that you are the temple of God,
and that the Spirit of God dwells in you?" (1 Cor 3:16).**

BAPTISMAL ROBES AND HARD-HATS

This seems to be a strange feast to displace the ordinary Sunday
liturgy. It does not celebrate any mystery of the life of Christ or of Mary
or even of any saint. Yet it is a day with great significance and history, a
commemoration of that church which is the episcopal seat of the Pope
as bishop of Rome and is called "the mother of all churches." For almost fifteen hundred years this church was for Catholics what the Vatican is today. Five ecumenical councils were held there between the
twelfth and sixteenth centuries. The name derives from its dedication
to St. John (apparently once the Evangelist and once the Baptist during
its many rebuildings) and from a gift of the estates of the Laterani
family to the pope by Constantine in A.D. 313.

The readings, however, do not speak of buildings but of what makes
of a building a church. In beautiful imagery Ezekiel speaks of the
temple as the place of God's presence from which flow blessings to the
world. In John's Gospel, as in all the Gospels, Jesus attacks the com-
mercialism of the temple, driving away merchants by shouting "Stop
making my Father's house a marketplace." When challenged for a sign
of his authority to clean house, Jesus says, "Destroy this temple and in
three days I will raise it up." Following the familiar Johannine technique
of naïve understanding leading to deeper truth, the temple authorities
say somewhat cynically, "This temple has been under construction for

132

forty-six years, and you will raise it up in three days?" The Evangelist then almost whispers to the audience that Jesus was talking about the temple of his risen body. The new "Father's house" is the risen presence of Jesus with his community.

Paul gives an image of the Church while writing to a Christian community squabbling over allegiance to different missionaries—Kephas, Apollo, or Paul himself (to name one of the major ones among the contentious Corinthians). The second reading comes just after Paul has proposed a model of cooperative rather than competitive ministry: The first comparison from farming recalls that one plants, another waters, but only God "causes the growth," so that "we are God's co-workers . . . God's field, God's building" (1 Cor 3:9).

Never shy about his own accomplishments, Paul then says that he was the "master builder" (today "architect" or "master of the works") who laid the foundation, upon which others should build, while subtly warning people that poor construction (e.g., rivalries) will destroy the building. For Paul the true foundation is really Jesus Christ, and switching metaphors with alacrity, Paul calls the community "the temple of God" (1 Cor 3:16) where the Holy Spirit dwells. Paul's images here anticipate his vision in 1 Corinthians 12 of a church with different gifts and different, interdependent ministries.

This feast presents a paradox. We celebrate a local church, the Pope's parish church, yet the seat of his universal pastoral care. The first pope to reside at the Lateran was from Africa (Pope Miltiades), and only now are the riches of the African churches being harvested. We recall what is now a beautiful basilica, yet realize that it is not the building that forms the people but the people who build the Church. Catholics often have pride in and affection for their local parish but realize that the Church is more than the parish. Often people both inside and outside the Church identify the Church with the Pope or the Roman Curia, and while every pope may image Paul's master builder, Jesus is the enduring foundation, and ultimately only God gives growth.

As I write these lines, a building outside my window is in its fifth month of construction. I watched it from its origin as a large cavity in the ground, through the pouring of the foundation, the raising of the walls, and now the completion of the roof. Paul's images come alive. A great variety of skills are required, along with an immense amount of hard work by people in hard-hats, young and old. We can think of our Church in this way. It came forth from an empty cavern, the tomb of Christ, and throughout history and wherever it rises up, it calls on the different gifts and hard work of diverse people. Along with their baptismal robes, God's people wear hard-hats.

PRAYING WITH SCRIPTURE

- Prayerfully think of how you have experienced God in different churches throughout your life.

- Reflect on Paul's words that you are truly the dwelling place of God.

- Put on your hard-hat and think of some ways that you can be a co-worker in God's building.

Thirty-Third Sunday in Ordinary Time

Readings: Dan 12:1-3; Ps 16:5, 8-11; Heb 10:11-14, 18;
Mark 13:24-32

"You will show me the path to life,
fullness of joys in your presence" (Ps 16:11).

WHEN THE END IS NOT THE END

As the days grow shorter and the trees become "bare ruin'd choirs, where late the sweet birds sang," (Shakespeare, Sonnet 132), the liturgical year winds down with images of the end of history. Daniel speaks of a time "unsurpassed in distress" but followed by a general resurrection of the dead, when those who "lead the many to justice / shall be like the stars forever" (12:3).

The gospel that concludes the Markan cycle of readings also comes at the end of Jesus' eschatological discourse, in which he predicts the destruction of the Temple and the return of the Son of Man in glory. Yet Jesus resists a timetable for these events and tells a parable about reading the signs of the times, for "of that day or hour, no one knows, neither the angels in heaven, nor the Son, but only the Father" (Mark 13:32).

As the much touted year 2000 drew to a close, we recall the apocalyptic predictions of computer meltdown, failed power plants, water and food shortage—all symbolized by the ominous Y2K. Yet these evanesced as the routine of ordinary life unfolded. Strangely we are not too different from Mark's community, which expected that Jesus would return in their lifetime to inaugurate the kind of reign of God envisioned by Daniel. Yet despite the cries among early Christians, "Our Lord, come" (cf. 1 Cor 16:21), Jesus did not return, and we exist "between the times," the time of the advent of Christ into the world and the time of return. Through prayer and ritual the liturgical cycle renews this experience every year.

One of the most puzzling aspects of today's gospel is Jesus' prediction that the generation of his hearers will not pass away until the return of the Son of Man and his claim that not even the Son but only the Father knows the day or hour of the final events. This conflicts with a later Christological perspective in which Jesus was "with God" prior to creation (John 1:1-2) and shares knowledge and being with the Father (John 10:30; 17:11). Mark rather emphasizes Jesus as "truly human." Mark's Jesus shares the uncertainty of human history, and he will later pray that the hour of suffering might pass from him (Mark 14:34), even as he promises that his words will endure forever. This promise of today's gospel has been fulfilled.

Often the hope of the return of Jesus can devolve into fantastic speculation about contemporary events heralding the end, or it is dismissed as irrelevant in a scientific age. Yet for the next three Sundays the Liturgy of the Word presents images of the endtime. These can sustain lives of faith in many ways. They present a view of human history from the end looking backward. If those who lead the many to justice shall shine like stars, the community that waits for the end is summoned to join those leaders now.

Mark offers to a persecuted community a vision of hope: wars, natural disasters, betrayal by family members which will be overcome when the Son of Man returns to gather in his loved ones. This is not simply "pie in the sky," a palliative for human suffering; it is a way of stating that those who suffer and die are not forgotten in God's eyes. The century just past has witnessed unprecedented evil and suffering in the Holocaust and in massive slaughters of whole populations, as well as the spread of famine and disease.

The view of history from the end presents a countervision. Though not described in detail in the readings today, this vision includes images of abundant food (Isa 25:5-7), vindication of innocent sufferers, and a reign of peace. The reigning of God that Jesus hopes for as his own ministry nears an end points back to his very first words in Mark's Gospel: "Change your hearts, for the reign of God is at hand" (author's translation). These "apocalyptic" gospels are a sign that our lives can be formed by the kind of world we envision, while we face a world we grieve over. Our hopes should shape our lives as powerfully as our faith and our love. If we hope for a future of justice and peace, we must read the signs of the times, so that this future may begin now.

PRAYING WITH SCRIPTURE

- Reflect on the reading from Daniel, asking God to renew your hope of life forever with your loved ones.

- Place before God your deepest personal hopes, as well as your hopes for the Church and society.

- What signs of the times should shape our lives today?

The Solemnity of
Our Lord Jesus Christ the King

Readings: Dan 7:13-14; Ps 93:1-2, 5; Rev 1:5-8; John 18:33b-37

"My kingdom does not belong to this world"
(John 18:36).

A KING IN DISGUISE

The liturgical year concludes with this relatively new feast, instituted by Pope Pius XI in 1925 to celebrate the jubilee year and the sixteenth centenary of the Council of Nicaea. It also affirmed the primacy of Christ in the face of rising nationalism and fascism. The scriptural motifs are similar to those of the Ascension: the exaltation and rule of Christ. Along with the readings from the Thirty-Third Sunday in Ordinary Time and the First Sunday of Advent, they look to the second coming of Christ in glory and complete the cycle of the mysteries of Christ from birth to unending reign.

Yet kingship evokes ambiguous responses today. Royal weddings and funerals attract millions of viewers enthralled by solemn ritual and ceremonial elegance more than by a sense of awe at the power of monarchy. Women, and most men, reject the patriarchal overtones of kingship, especially in a nation that was founded in revolt from a king. Yet the readings are rife with the paradox that the kingship celebrated is in direct opposition to either outmoded or dominant claims to power.

Written in a time of severe persecution, the book of Daniel celebrates the enthronement of "one like a son of man" (lit.: "one in human form"), in contrast to the crumbling powers of the world empires. Daniel later indicates that this human one symbolizes the vindication of the "holy people of the Most High," the suffering people (Dan 7:27). The gospel presents one of the most dramatic scenes in the New Testament, in which an arrogant Pilate learns ironically that Jesus is a king, but not the kind he can deal with. When asked if he is a king, Jesus does not claim the title "king" but replies, "My kingdom does not belong to this world" (John 18:36). This does not mean that Jesus has proclaimed and enacted a purely spiritual or otherworldly kingdom, but that his present and future reign does not operate according to the world's criteria of power and dominance.

Jesus further redefines his kingship as being a witness to the truth. The words "truth" and "true," used thirty-nine times in John, are multivalent terms with overtones of "non-concealment," disclosure of God's wisdom and plan of salvation and the reliability of Jesus' words. Jesus speaks the truth about God and humanity, which humans can reject, as "the way, the truth and the life," and accepting such truth brings true freedom (8:32). When faced with the truth of Jesus, people in John's Gospel must choose to believe or reject Jesus. Pilate here becomes the parade example of the "fence-sitter," who can at best muster a cynical response to Jesus, "What is truth?" (18:38, unfortunately omitted from today's reading). He is a person who, "having failed to listen to the truth and decide in its favor [so that] he [and] all who would imitate him inevitably finish in the service of the world" (R. E. Brown, *John*, Anchor Bible, p. 864).

To celebrate Christ as King is to enter into the deepest mysteries of faith. Jesus, bound and seemingly powerless before Pilate, the symbol of a powerful empire that holds the scales of life and death, is the true King who possesses the power to grant a life that never ends. All who belong to the truth will be followers of this King and will hear his voice. This truth is not revealed in dominating power but by suffering witnesses.

This gospel summons to decision not only Pilate but the Church today as well. Johannine truth suggests an authenticity between belief and practice, a faithful witness that embodies the teaching of the Johannine Jesus. John's Jesus is "the friend" who gives his life for others and washes their feet as a symbol of that loving service they are to embody. He is the Good Shepherd who not only seeks the lost, as in the Synoptic Gospels, but lays down his life for the sheep. Jesus' kingdom does not belong to this world because it rejects the way of violence (18:36) and domination and the pretensions that mask truth. Pilate stands before Jesus and asks, "What is truth?" As people stand before the Church today, will they ask the same question?

PRAYING WITH SCRIPTURE

- What images does Jesus as "King" evoke for you? How does the gospel challenge these images?

- Jesus comes to testify to the truth. Pray about how you may also be a witness to the truth.

- Where today must we listen to the voice of Christ?

APPENDIX

The following Sundays do not occur in 2002–2003 but are included here for possible use in a future year that uses Cycle B. The feasts of the Transfiguration and All Saints are not transferred to Sunday.

Fourth Sunday in Ordinary Time

Readings: Deut 18:15-20; Ps 95:1-2, 6-9; 1 Cor 7:32-35; Mark 1:21-28

"What is this? A new teaching with authority" (Mark 1:27).

A SHOCKING BEGINNING

Immediately after calling the first disciples, Jesus inaugurates his ministry with a paradigmatic day foreshadowing the rest of the Gospel (Mark 1:21-34), comprising exorcisms and healings that crystallize John's prediction of the arrival of the stronger one. This first story reflects contemporary Jewish thought that the advent of God's reign would spell the defeat of evil, which is personified in an array of demons and unclean spirits. From the rebuke of the demon and its expulsion by a single command, readers know that Jesus, who will later be charged with being in league with Satan (Mark 3:22) and who is condemned as a blasphemer (14:64), is a victor over evil—which in turn underscores the authority of Jesus as teacher. His word is so powerful that people abandon their occupations and follow him, and even demonic powers cower before it.

The Old Testament readings today, as on virtually every Sunday, are determined by the gospel. The brief reading from Jonah describes the second call of Jonah to preach repentance to the Ninevites. Reading the whole book is rewarding, since Jonah, rare among biblical narratives, garbs a profound theological message in humor. Jonah is called to go east to preach to the Ninevites but rather heads as far west as possible, boards a ship, only to be thrown overboard in a great storm, but is miraculously coughed up on dry land by the most famous whale in history (again, somewhat comedic, since sea monsters are supposed to gobble people up—Jer 51:34).

When Jonah finally follows God's command, all of Nineveh repents; even the cattle are clothed in sackcloth—which saddens Jonah, since any self-respecting prophet would expect Nineveh to be destroyed (Nah 1:1-4). God then instructs Jonah—and ourselves—that universal divine mercy embraces even the most feared enemy. Another prophetic motif is sounded by Deuteronomy 18:15-20 with the expectation of a prophet like Moses, who was not only a great lawgiver but a figure of power. Like Jesus, he confronted the forces of evil, liberated his people from slavery, and enacted a covenant in blood (Exod 24:8; Mark 14:24).

The readings for these first Sundays of Ordinary Time offer a kaleidoscope of themes: the graphic realism of Mark's Jesus; the sudden coming of God into ordinary human life; the challenge for the Church to be prophetic, and a "community of disciples" (Pope John Paul II); the confrontation of God's reign with the anti-reign of evil. Yet, viewed through the prism of Jonah, the deeper message may be that conversion, community, and confrontation with evil are ultimately God's doing, achieved in startling ways.

PRAYING WITH SCRIPTURE

- Jesus begins his ministry by forming communities and immediately confronts the power of evil. Pray over ways that the Christian community may confront destructive forces in human life.

- God raised up prophets like Moses and sent Jesus like a prophet. Pray that prophets may arise in our midst today. Reflect on people whom you would call prophets.

Ninth Sunday in Ordinary Time

Readings: Deut 5:12-15; Ps 81:3-8, 10-11; 2 Cor 4:6-11;
Mark 22:23–3:6

> **"Take care to keep holy the sabbath day as the LORD,
> your God, commanded you" (Deut 5:12).**

REST AND REPENTS

As Lent approaches, this Sunday concludes the continuous reading
of Mark, which will not resume until the first week of July. The gospel
portrays two Sabbath controversies, which end with the plot of Pharisees and Herodians to "destroy" Jesus, an anticipation of the Passion, a
helpful lead-in to the Lenten season.

The reading from Deuteronomy lays out the legislation for the Sabbath rest from work for all people, including "slaves" and "aliens" in
remembrance of the people's liberation from Egypt, where they too
had been slaves and aliens. In other passages the Sabbath rest is also
a commemoration of the divine "rest" from creative activity on the
seventh day (Gen 2:1-3) crystallized in the Fourth Commandment of
the Decalogue (Exod 20:8-11). The Sabbath is a day of rest from all work
in order to celebrate and remember God as Creator and Liberator.

This double significance of the Sabbath provides the tension in the
gospel readings. In two places Jesus offends Pharisees by seeming to
violate the Sabbath rest when he provides food for his disciples and
heals a man on the Sabbath. The Pharisees were known for their dedicated and strict observance of the Law by creating a great number of
prescriptions that formed a fence around the Law, guarding it from any
direct transgressions. These disputes do not represent an attack on Judaism but an inner-Jewish debate in which Jesus invokes the liberating
meaning of the Sabbath against a strict interpretation of the command
to rest. Both responses of Jesus are summarized in the ringing cry "The
Sabbath was made for humans, and not humans for the Sabbath" (my

translation). The Sabbath rest prescribed in Deuteronomy was to provide an opportunity to all people, including the most marginal in society, to recall God's liberating love for suffering humans. Jesus as "Son of Man," who will ultimately give his life as a "ransom" for others (Mark 10:45), gives a new dimension to the Sabbath rest.

These readings present a prophetic challenge to the Church today. The Sabbath (Sunday) rest has virtually disappeared in our mercantile society as the day becomes simply another occasion to "shop until you drop." Today those most likely to be forced to work on Sunday are among the most vulnerable in our society, immigrants (the resident alien of the Bible), single parents, poor service workers. Far from absolving contemporary Christians from Sabbath obligations, Jesus' actions herald the true observance of the Sabbath as an occasion to create time for God, to think of the vulnerable in our midst, and to counter individually and collectively the destruction of the "Lord's day."

PRAYING WITH SCRIPTURE

- Spend time on a Sunday thinking of the day's deeper meaning. Recall the gifts of creation and of God's saving love.

- In the days leading up to Lent, step back, take a second look, and ask how best to "walk the walk."

Tenth Sunday in Ordinary Time

Readings: Gen 3:9-15; Ps 130:1-8; 2 Cor 4:13–5:1; Mark 3:20-35

> **"Out of the depths I cry to you, O LORD;**
> **LORD, hear my voice!" (Ps 130:1).**

VOICES FROM THE GRAVE!

One of the most powerful books I have ever read, sadly out of print, is *Dying We Live,* a collection written by prisoners in Nazi Germany on the verge of execution. The authors range from an ordinary farm boy who refused to join the S.S. through world-recognized martyrs such as Edith Stein, Alfred Delp, S.J., and Dietrich Bonhoeffer. They include Catholic and non-Catholic clergy and religious and a combination of people from leading German families, along with ordinary but courageous people, for example, Marie Kuderikova, a factory worker, and Heidi Coppi, who gave birth to her first child shortly before her execution. Amid intimations of terror, fear, and loneliness terms of endearment echo through the letters: "my dear little Mama," "my dearest, my good Tim," "dear, dear, dear Aneli." Yet a chorus of beautiful notes arise to God: concern over the pain caused to loved ones by their sentences; trust and hope; the need to resist the demonic evil of Nazism, and prayers for persecutors. We hear the essence of Christianity voiced from the silence of the death chambers.

The book title echoes St. Paul's profound reflection on the cost and course of discipleship, "always carrying about in the body the dying of Jesus, so that the life of Jesus may also be manifest in our body" (2 Cor 4:10). Though Paul would himself suffer martyrdom a few years after writing this letter, his ministry in Corinth involved great suffering. After founding the community, Paul dealt with a host of pastoral problems in his first letter to the Corinthians: partisan disputes; a range of sexual problems; controversies over the celebration of the liturgy and over prophetic gifts, along with a confused theology of the resurrection. Far from assuaging all the problems, a few years later Corinth seethes with a new set of problems that cause Paul great anguish and suffering.

A group whom Paul calls "super-apostles" (2 Cor 11:4-5) arrives preaching what Paul thinks is "another" Gospel. They pride themselves on their rhetorical gifts and mock Paul as not up to their standard. Paul responds not by direct attack as much as by constantly pointing to the real source of his strength. Relying on the grace of God, Paul states that "power is made perfect in weakness" (2 Cor 12:9) and throughout the letter draws on his own personal experience of grace and power amid suffering as a sign of the true gospel. Today's reading from Paul concludes one such list where Paul has expressed the paradox of "dying we live," and not only for the present but for "an eternal weight of glory beyond all comparison" (2 Cor 4:17).

The gospel also touches on themes echoing through the letters from Hitler's prisons. It begins with Jesus misunderstood by his loved ones, who think he is out of his mind and want to take him home quietly. Then a group of scribes appear and charge that because he expels demons he must be in league with demons. Jesus responds with three short parabolic examples that underscore the absurdity of the divided reign or household of Satan allowing internal division, and concludes with the crux of the argument: he is the stronger one who, by his exorcisms, has entered Satan's house and plundered it.

Jesus then utters the ominous statement about the unforgivable sin. All sin and even blasphemy will be forgiven, but not blasphemy against the Holy Spirit, which "will never have forgiveness." This sin, which seems so contrary to God's mercy, has evoked a mountain of interpretation and application through the ages. Augustine exercised a major influence by describing it as final impenitence and resistance to God's grace, which was taken up by both Catholics and Protestants. In Mark, however, it is not final impenitence or refusal to accept doctrine but a deliberate choice to interpret the presence of goodness and divine action as evil. This is the "sin" committed by movements like Nazism, which demonize and kill those who truly speak God's will to the world.

The final section of the Gospel returns to Jesus and his family. Still concerned about his strange actions, his mother and brothers want him to come with them. In reply, Jesus shouts, "Who are my mother and brothers?" and utters the extraordinary words, "Here are my mother and brothers. For whoever does the will of God is my brother and sister and mother." The shadow of the cross falls over this scene, since the way to the cross is the will of God followed by Jesus (Mark 14:35-36). Even the most intimate of family relationships, that of Jesus to his mother, must yield to the demands of God's will.

The letters from *Dying We Live* are a virtual commentary on today's readings, but they are not just voices from the past. The paradox of power made perfect in weakness is alive in the Church today. Resistance to demonic power is as pertinent today as it was during the Nazi times. Powerful governments and institutions cloak themselves in the mantle of legal and often religious respectability and condemn those who resist them as false prophets, thus replaying the sin against the Holy Spirit. Seeking and following the will of God can bring divisions among family and loved ones. Paul expressed the most profound mystery of Christian faith when he was attacked; and the new family created by Jesus is one which does his Father's will. A close Jesuit friend of mine from Latin America who himself opposed evil power prior to his early death once told me that the U.S. Church was too prosperous and complacent and might benefit from a persecution or two. He may have been right. Were the voices from Hitler's prisons right?

PRAYING WITH SCRIPTURE

- Imagine yourself condemned to death for an act of resistance to evil and write a letter to one of your loved ones.

- During times of misunderstanding by family and friends, converse with Jesus as he appears in today's gospel.

- Pray over particular challenges that face you in seeking God's will.

Eleventh Sunday in Ordinary Time

Readings: Ezek 17:22-24; Ps 92:2-3, 13-16; 2 Cor 5:6-10;
Mark 4:26-34

"Of its own accord the land yields fruit" (Mark 4:28).

AN APPOINTED TIME FOR EVERYTHING!

I can still remember the Second World War. It was often a fearful time, but for a nine-year-old a paradoxically exciting time. I recall ominous reports on the evening news by Gabriel Heater, "Ah there's bad news tonight." It was a time of growing together as a family: standing in lines with my mother at the market to buy meat; reading letters from cousins with the Army and Air Force in Europe, preparing air raid shelters, and listening to exhortations for those at home to collect scrap metal and grow victory gardens.

Though we were city folk, one early spring day my father decided to tear up our back yard and plant a garden. No longer would I toss a tennis ball and dare my dog Twinkle to find it behind the large lilac bush. With great eagerness the family became urban farmers, and that spring we planted tomato seeds, corn, beans, and peas. During the languid Baltimore summer, like the farmer in today's parable, we went to bed and got up day after day and watched our handiwork sprout, grow, and flourish. (Our tomatoes were the envy of the neighborhood.) It was a wonderful experience of the mystery and beauty of nature's bounty.

In the gospel today, Jesus, no city boy but from a small rural town in Galilee, takes images from his early years to portray the mystery of God's reign, that is, the mystery of God's power being made manifest in his ministry. In the first parable a rather unconcerned farmer just scatters the seed, resumes a restful life, and the seed sprouts and grows; how, he doesn't know. This action of the sower seems a bit strange, since in an earlier parable (Mark 4:1-10) Jesus speaks of the perils of agriculture. Yet here the seed grows on its own, and the farmer returns only to harvest.

What was Jesus trying to say in the parable? Perhaps many things. To those of his followers who expected the kingdom to blossom forth immediately he may be cautioning that God's times are not human times. To others who wanted to hurry the arrival of the kingdom by violent or extraordinary means, the parable says that God's reign has a power of its own. To both groups the stress is on being ready for the harvest. A time will come to act, and we must stand ready.

The second parable is one of hope and contrast. The reigning of God is like a mustard seed, which is the smallest of all seeds but which springs up and grows into the largest of plants, so that (somewhat hyperbolically) the birds of the sky can dwell in its branches. Though this is a parable about the contrast between insignificant beginnings and extravagant results, it has other dimensions. Using similar imagery, Ezekiel consoles an exiled people with the hope that they too will again become a majestic cedar, and birds of every kind will dwell beneath it. Ezekiel chooses the familiar image in antiquity of trees as powerful kingdoms which overshadow their subjects. Yet humor and irony characterize Jesus' use of this image. It is not the crest of a mighty cedar that will be replanted and flourish, but an insignificant mustard seed, and the reign he proclaims is not a "majestic cedar" but a mustard bush, which still shelters "the birds of the sky." The mustard plant has also a certain disconcerting quality; it is very hearty and tends to take over a garden, attracting birds which can destroy the rest of the garden. Jesus images a kingdom not like a lofty cedar, which reflects the structures of power of ancient empires, but a rather bothersome bush, which still provides a haven for even unwanted birds.

These parables suggest ways for reflecting on the kingdom today. God's reigning or kingdom is precisely that; it is God's doing, not human effort. Despite certain popular hymns, in the New Testament no human ever "builds" the kingdom of God. God's reign is a power that affects life in strange and wonderful ways, but we, like the farmer, often "know not how." Like the mustard seed, it evokes hope that from insignificant beginnings startling results may follow. The history of some of the greatest movements in the Church, such as the founding of religious communities or forms of the lay apostolate, is a story of fragile beginnings and extraordinary results. Also like the mustard bush, these movements often seem to take over vested territory and attract and shelter in their branches some very pesky birds.

Praying with Scripture

- Pray about ways that various forms of growth have taken place in your lives, often in ways that you "know not how."

- Quietly contemplate the beauty of nature and pray with the psalmist, "It is good to give thanks to the LORD" (Ps 92:2).

- Reflect with hope on how small beginnings may bear the promise of startling results.

Twelfth Sunday in Ordinary Time

Readings: Job 38:1, 8-11; Ps 107:23-26, 28-31; 2 Cor 5:14-17;
Mark 4:35-41

"These saw the works of the LORD
and his wonders in the abyss" (Ps 107:24).

COME SAIL WITH ME!

From time immemorial "the sea" has been not only a source of teeming life but an arena of struggle and conflict. Ancient Mesopotamian myths speak of the sea monster Tiamat, and Canaanite mythology speaks of Lotan, a sea monster vanquished by Ba`al, reflected in the biblical accounts of the struggle with Leviathan (Job 41:1; Ps 74:14; 104:26). Ancient epics such as the *Odyssey* and the *Aeneid* revel in stories of perilous sea journeys, as does the biblical story of Jonah and the final voyage of Paul in Acts 27. Today "sea adventures" are sure box office hits: *Titanic; The Perfect Storm; The Poseidon Adventure,* along with classic literary works such as *Moby Dick, The Old Man and the Sea* and "The Wreck of the Deutschland," by Gerard Manley Hopkins. Fascination with such stories may spring from a deep consciousness that the "chaos monster," or inner turmoil of humanity lurks below an often calm surface.

Today's gospel presents the first of many Markan sea voyages where Jesus travels from the western (Jewish) side of the Lake of Galilee (which Mark calls "the sea") to the eastern (Gentile) side. The sea is a boundary separating the two sides, which Jesus bridges, and Mark carefully notes that Jesus performs similar powerful works on each side of the lake: healings; exorcisms; the feeding of first five thousand and then four thousand. Theologically Mark says that Jesus comes to bring the benefits of God's reign to both Jew and non-Jew. As a conclusion to the parable discourse of Mark 4, the victory over the raging sea shows Jesus as powerful in word and in deed.

The narrative is concise and vivid. The disciples take Jesus into the boat, most likely similar to the "Kinneret boat," discovered in 1986, which is roughly twenty-six feet long and eight feet wide. Immediately a violent squall, most likely a tornado-like windstorm, hits the voyagers, and the boat seems in danger of being swamped. Jesus is sleeping, which recalls the sower of 4:27; an untroubled sleep in the Old Testament is a sign of trust in the power and protection of God (Prov 3:32-34; Pss 3:5; 4:8; Job 11:18-19). The ironic contrast between the raging sea, the terror of the disciples, and the deep sleep of Jesus heightens the power and word of Jesus.

The disciples rouse Jesus with a pleading cry, which is similar to the cry of the crew in another biblical sea miracle, that of Jonah when the non-Jewish crew cries to the God of Israel, "Lord, do not let us perish." The description of Jesus standing suggests rising to his full height in the stern of the boat confronting the raging waters, which he then "rebukes," (a term often used in exorcisms, e.g., 1:25; 3:12, as in his specific command, "Quiet! Be Still!"). The furious storm is both embodiment and symbol of the power of evil. The sea immediately is tranquil, which again mirrors the following exorcism, when an equally violent and out-of-control demoniac sits calmly in his right mind. Both victories over evil cause awe and fear (Mark 4:41; 5:15).

The focus of the story then shifts from Jesus' power over the sea as he turns to the disciples whom he has just rescued from mortal danger. He asks why they are terrified, using a Greek adjective that suggests not simply fear but cowardice, and then rebukes them for their lack of faith. Their reaction and fear is surprising, since from the beginning of their time with Jesus they have seen him as the powerful one who casts out demons and heals the sick. The rebuke of Jesus is harsh: "Do you not yet have faith?"

The calming of the sea has many dimensions. It stresses that God's power, which was manifest in defeating the "sea monsters," is present in Jesus. Mark's readers, buffeted by the storms of persecution under Nero or the chaos caused by the Jewish War and the destruction of the Temple, are urged to realize that Jesus is with them, but that the deeper threat is loss of faith and courage. As early as St. Hippolytus, the boat became a symbol of the Church beaten by the waves but not submerged. As we move from first-century Galilee to our world, we see also many local churches beaten by storms of hatred and persecution where people call out "we are perishing." Yet we hear also stories of faith and courage which exceed that of the faltering disciples in Mark. The raging sea for others today is a symbol of the emotional or personal chaos that seems about to overwhelm their lives, and yet in their moments of doubt they may be brought to say with the disciples, "Who then is this whom even the wind and sea obey?"

PRAYING WITH SCRIPTURE

- In moments when life seems overwhelming, place yourself in the boat with the disciples and pray, "Teacher, do you not care that we are perishing?"

- Pray with the beleaguered Church in parts of the world such as India, Sudan, and Indonesia.

- Job heard God's voice "out of the storm." Where do we hear God's voice today?

Thirteenth Sunday in Ordinary Time

Readings: Wis 1:13-15; 2:23-24; Ps 30:2, 4-6, 11-13; 2 Cor 8:7, 9, 13-15; Mark 5:21-43

"I will extol you, O Lord, for you drew me clear"
(Ps 30:2).

TWO LIVES RESTORED

Today's readings offer two of the most vivid miracle stories of the Gospel. Through the familiar technique of "sandwiching," two stories are interwoven in a way that enriches both.

The narrative begins with Jairus, a synagogue official who throws himself at the feet of Jesus, begging him to heal his daughter, who is near death. Jesus goes off with Jairus, and the second story begins. In the crowd is a woman whose suffering Mark vividly describes. She has been afflicted for twelve years "with a hemorrhage," most likely some form of vaginal bleeding that ancient medical writers describe as involving great suffering from both the malady and its treatment. She has spent all she had on physicians without any improvement (sounds hauntingly contemporary) and is growing worse. Yet she is a woman of faith and courage and moves through the crowd to touch Jesus.

When she touches him, she is "immediately" healed, only to hear Jesus ask, "Who has touched my clothes?" Perhaps fearing a rebuke, she comes "in fear and trembling," only to hear Jesus' words: "Daughter, your faith has saved you. Go in peace." Salvation and peace are both the actual physical healing and the gifts of the messianic age.

The first story resumes with the report of the death of Jairus' daughter and Jesus' commands, "Do not be afraid; just have faith," reminiscent of the faith embodied in the woman just healed. After a short and vivid description of the wailing mourners, Jesus says, improbably, "The child is not dead but asleep," and the mourning turns to ridicule. With great tenderness Jesus then brings the child's parents, enters the room, takes

155

the dead child by the hand, and says simply, "Little girl, I say to you, arise." The young woman "arose immediately and walked around." There is then the interesting note that she was twelve years old, which provides the key to the linking of the two stories, since the woman in the crowd had suffered for twelve years.

In the culture of that time twelve was thought to be the marriageable age. The "little girl," then, has died before she could become a wife and mother. The woman had suffered an illness that prevented her from bearing children. Jesus not only rescued these women from death but restores to them their life-giving capacity. Both can bring forth life from their bodies, one racked with disease, the other deprived of life itself. Bringing forth children was seen in Judaism as an imitation of the life-giving power of God and a fulfillment of the command to make the earth fruitful.

The Jesus who emerges from these stories is one who is compassionate in the face of human suffering and who makes the needs of these sufferers the norm for his action, to the disregard of social taboos and conventions. He talks to a woman in public and violates the stringent taboo against touching a corpse.

Faith, especially as embodied by the bleeding woman, can exist in the face of seemingly hopeless situations. These narratives also challenge the Church universal to recognize the courageous faith of women and to be on the side of women, whose human dignity and ability to give and sustain life are threatened by war, disease, abuse, and poverty.

Praying with Scripture

- Stand with the woman suffering from long-term illness and ask for the grace of similar courage and faith.

- Pray in gratitude for the gifts of women to the contemporary Church and think of how the Church may imitate better the life-giving actions of Jesus.

The Transfiguration of the Lord

Readings: Dan 7:9-10, 13-14; Ps 97:1-2, 5-6, 9; 2 Pet 1:16-19;
Mark 9:2-10

> **"The heavens proclaim his justice;**
> **all peoples see his glory" (Ps 97:6).**

WHAT PRICE GLORY?

This Sunday repeats the gospel for the Second Sunday of Lent, while the first two readings are selected for the feast. Though celebrated from the fifth century in the Eastern Church, the Transfiguration was introduced into the Western calendar only in 1457 to celebrate the victory over the Turks at Belgrade (not recommended as a topic for homilies). The gospel recounts a vision given to the disciples of the transformed Jesus in conversation with Moses and Elijah and the sound of a heavenly voice proclaiming divine approval of "my beloved Son." It serves as a message of hope to earthly disciples who have just heard Jesus proclaim his coming death by crucifixion.

The reading from Daniel provides another vision of such hope. Though narrated as an event in the reign of Belshazzar, the last king of Babylon, this section of Daniel reflects the persecution of the Jewish people under Antiochus IV, Epiphanes ("divine manifestation"), in 167–64 B.C. In 7:1-8, Daniel interprets the king's dream of four great beasts, which symbolize the succession of the four empires of the Babylonians, Medes, Persians, and Greeks, with the final vision heralding the destruction of Antiochus IV. Today's reading depicts a session of the heavenly court and the granting of power by "the Ancient One" (God) to one "like a Son of Man," who approaches the Ancient One on the clouds of heaven and receives "dominion, glory, and kingship."

This section of Daniel had immense influence on the New Testament and is the source of the repeated self-description of Jesus as Son of Man, as well as the source of an avalanche of scholarly studies debating the identity of "one like a Son of man" in Daniel. One convincing interpretation is that the figure stands for the persecuted "holy people of the Most High," (Dan 7:27) those Jews who suffered martyrdom rather than apostatize under Antiochus and who also receive an everlasting kingdom. Thus interpreted, the narrative serves as a beacon of hope to a persecuted people that they will be vindicated.

Ironically, then, for a feast that originally celebrated a military victory, the theology of both Daniel and Mark is distinctly pacifist. History is under the control of God, who approves the way of suffering of his beloved Son, who dies under imperial edict. The mightiest of empires will fall, while those who die as martyrs will reign with God. The Transfiguration therefore has a special significance today, when we think of the many "martyrs for justice" of recent decades, such as Martin Luther King Jr., Oscar Romero, the religious men and women of El Salvador, the silenced martyrs in China, and countless others known only as "the people of the holy ones." Empires exercise brutal power, but they fade, while the hope of a transformed humanity remains.

PRAYING WITH SCRIPTURE

- Remember in prayer people who have given their lives as witnesses to God's power and glory even amid persecution.

- Pray in gratitude when you have felt the transforming presence of God that provided hope in your journey of following Christ.

Twenty-Fourth Sunday in Ordinary Time

Readings: Isa 50:4c-9a; Ps 116:1-6, 8-9; Jas 2:14-18; Mark 8:27-35

**"What good is it if someone says he has faith
but does not have works?" (Jas 2:14).**

THE COST OF DISCIPLESHIP

The readings touch on the most profound mysteries of Christianity: why do the innocent suffer, why must the followers of Jesus deny themselves and take up their crosses? The first reading presents the third of the four Servant Songs (see Isa 42:1-4; 49:1-7; 50:4-11; 52:13–53:12), which expresses the motif of the suffering just person who is foolish by human standards but who is accepted by God (Job; Wis 2:12-24).

The gospel comes at a watershed in Mark, when Jesus begins his "way" to Jerusalem and to his cross (8:27–10:45). Mark has artfully composed this section by bracketing it with two narratives about the healing of blind people. In the first (8:22-26) the blind man recovers his sight gradually, while in the second (10:46-52) the healed Bartimaeus jumps up and follows Jesus "on the way." This whole section is structured around three declarations of Jesus that he must suffer and die, followed by three misunderstandings on the part of the disciples, which evoke further teaching on discipleship. The stories of the blind people are symbolic of the gradual growth in understanding that is to lead to following Jesus on the way of the cross.

The gospel today contains two sections, the messianic confession of Peter and the prediction of the Passion followed by misunderstanding and teaching. Jesus begins by asking, "Who do people say that I am," and the disciples offer various common opinions. He then goes on to ask, "But who do you say that I am?" Peter, the first disciple called, immediately responds, "You are the Christ," that is, God's anointed bearer of salvation. This evokes from Jesus a strong command not to tell anyone. Mark follows immediately with the prediction of the Passion, foretelling that the Son of Man, a powerful figure in the first part of the Gospel (2:10, 28) must be rejected, suffer, die, and rise again. Peter then takes him aside and "began to rebuke him" (the verb used earlier when Jesus silences demons, 3:12, or calms the raging sea, 4:39). With consummate irony, Mark then notes that Jesus "rebuked Peter" in turn (the same verb) and called Peter "Satan." Peter's failure is that "you are thinking not as God does, but as human beings do."

The following verses provide God's thoughts on suffering, couched in the universalized form "whoever wishes to come after me." These hard sayings—on denying one's very self, taking up the cross and losing one's life if one wants to save it—are a challenge not simply to the called disciples but to anyone who wants to follow Jesus on the way. Since Mark was written within vivid memory of both the horrors of the Jewish War against Rome and the persecution under Nero, when Christians were used as torches to light Nero's garden, such predictions were tragically fulfilled in the community, but with the hope that such loss was paradoxically saving one's life by being joined with the risen Son of Man.

These readings offer rich and sober material for reflection. The pointed question of Jesus, "Who do you say that I am?" cuts to the heart of Christianity. Amid the welter of contemporary opinions, each person must answer this question, and not simply once but amid the changing currents and circumstances of life. Especially shocking is Peter's failure, culminating in his virtual apostasy in 14:71, when, after being with Jesus almost every moment of his public life, he states, "I do not know this man about whom you are talking." Such a picture of Peter may have been especially consoling to the Roman community, which experienced apostasy and betrayal during Nero's persecution yet knew that Peter died a faithful disciple. It also provided strong motivation for reconciliation with the "betrayers" in the community, and can do so today in those manifold situations where peace and reconciliation must follow appalling internal wars and slaughter.

The call to take up one's cross has served as the clarion call for martyrdom, as Pope John Paul II pointed out on May 7, 1997, in the Roman Colosseum at an ecumenical ceremony honoring thousands of martyrs: "Where hatred seemed to corrupt the whole of life, leaving no escape from its logic, they proved that 'love is stronger than death,'" and "proclaimed their loyalty to Christ crucified and risen."

While voluntary martyrdom has been the glory of Christianity, it is difficult to think of the unwanted suffering of the innocent as willed by a loving God. The Jesus who predicts his resurrection must be paired with Jesus, racked by fear, who prays that his Father take away the cup and who dies with a cry of abandonment. Jesus speaks of "taking one's cross," not of imposing it on others. Nor is suffering a punishment for sin or a sign of self-neglect. God did not spare his beloved Son pain and death. Pastorally, when confronted by shocking suffering, people often cannot hear the word of the cross; hopefully, they may come to realize that they do not suffer alone. Christianity does not solve the mystery of why people suffer but offers guidance on how cross-bearing can take place. Even Jesus ended his life with another helping him to carry his cross (Mark 15:21).

PRAYING WITH SCRIPTURE

- In prayer respond to the question, "Who do you say that I am?"

- Pray about occasions when you have experienced that love is stronger than suffering and death.

- Think of ways in which you can help to carry the crosses of suffering people today (see especially James 2:14-18).

All Saints

Readings: Rev 7:2-4, 9-14; Ps 24:1-6; 1 John 3:1-3; Matt 5:1-12a

"Beloved, we are God's children now" (1 John 3:2).

WHAT ME, A SAINT!

As the days shorten and the beautiful autumn colors begin to fade, the Church reminds us of both the splendor and frailty of Christian life. Goodness and love of God and neighbor in the lives of countless and nameless holy ones have illumined our way, but they have departed as we commemorate the feasts of All Saints and All Souls *(el Dia de los Muertos)*. Last Sunday we celebrated one of the little people, Bartimaeus, who followed Jesus on the way; today we celebrate the succession of the saints, that "great multitude, which no one could count" (Rev 7:9).

Though we think of saints today as models of virtue signaled by elaborate canonization ceremonies, in Acts and Paul "saint" is used as virtual synonym for a member of the Christian community, even of communities like Corinth (1 Cor 1:1) that, by our standards, embraced those with less than heroic virtue (squabbling about power, engaged in strange sexual behavior, fighting over the liturgy). The gospel proclaims Jesus' inaugural sermon, which heralds those paradoxical attitudes that bring blessing and happiness before God. Strangely blessed and happy are people who are marginal, grieving, or non-violent and those who hunger and die for a just world, along with those who bring consolation and peace—in short, all the saints.

Matthew's Beatitudes constitute Jesus' platform for election to God's kingdom. As our own election nears, we are sated with platforms, programs, promises, and an overdose of platitudes. But we must ask ourselves who cares about the kind of people envisioned by the Beatitudes. These are the new silent majority, yet it is this majority, silent among us or silent in death, whose enduring presence we memorialize these days.

Praying with Scripture

- Pray in gratitude for those "little people" and unnamed saints, with us and departed, who have been your companions on the way of discipleship.

- Pray over the Beatitudes and think of those values that should inform your election choices.

Thirty-First Sunday in Ordinary Time

Readings: Deut 6:2-6; Ps 18:2-4, 47, 51; Heb 7:23-28; Mark 12:28b-34

> **"Take to heart these words which I enjoin
> on you today" (Deut 6:6).**

BACK TO BASICS

People often wonder, "What does it mean to be a good Catholic?" A cacophony of voices shouts answers: go to Mass every Sunday; obey the teaching of the Pope; be concerned about the poor and about injustice in the world; experience the gifts of God's Spirit. In an age of hyper-communication Catholics are drowned by a torrent of catechisms, creeds, papal documents, letters from local bishops, pronouncements from the Vatican, along with confusing interpretations of all of the above in the public media.

In today's gospel Jesus confronts a similar situation. A scribe, a specialist in the Law, asks Jesus, "Which is the first of all the commandments?" For Jews of that period, God's love for the people was revealed in the Sinai covenant and in observing "all his statutes and ordinances" (Deut 6:2). By Jesus' time these had been codified into six hundred thirteen prohibitions or commands. The question of the scribe is genuine. Jesus then responds by quoting the same Torah (covenant law) that the scribe so ardently studied. He cites the opening verses of the Shema, "Hear, O Israel," (Deut 6:4-9; 11:13-21; Num 15:37-41), recited every day by all Jews, summoning the people to total love of God with heart, mind, soul and strength, a love that springs out of gratitude for what God has done for them.

Citing another text from the Torah, Jesus then says that the second command is "You shall love your neighbor as yourself" (Lev 19:18). Though in Leviticus the neighbor is primarily another Israelite, by the time of Jesus it included non-Jews. In first-century Jewish thought, "as yourself," means "as though he or she were yourself" or as if you were in the same situation as your neighbor. This is a variation of Jesus'

Golden Rule, "Do to others whatever you would have them do to you," which is similar to a saying of the first-century Rabbi Hillel, "What is hateful to yourself, do not do to your neighbor; this is the whole law, the rest is commentary" (Babylonian Talmud). Today the neighbor may be as near as one's spouse or as distant as a homeless person huddled around a heating vent in the depth of winter.

In our somewhat therapeutic culture, the phrase "as yourself" is often presented as if a healthy self-love is a prerequisite to love of neighbor. Love of neighbor may be extremely difficult for a person undergoing great suffering or one who has been seriously wounded, but its fundamental presupposition is not psychological well-being, but a conviction well expressed by Thomas Merton: "The beginning of the fight against hatred, the basic Christian answer to hatred, is not the commandment to love but what must necessarily come before in order to make the commandment bearable and comprehensible. It is a prior commandment to believe. The root of Christian love is not the will to love, but the faith that one is loved . . . by God although unworthy or rather irrespective of one's worth!"

Both love of God and of neighbor were not expressed only by prayer and confession; they were enshrined in daily life. Jesus and other first-century Jews prayed at least three times a day, observed the Sabbath as remembrance of God's creative love, and recalled the saving deeds of God in a cycle of feasts (Sabbath, Passover, Pentecost, Tabernacles, Day of Atonement). The Qumran scrolls show that love of neighbor was to be translated into action: "Each one to love his brother [or sister] as himself [or herself], and to support the needy, the poor and the stranger" (Damascus Document).

The Gospels portray a Jesus whose love of God and neighbor was translated into action by teaching his Father's mercy, by healing touches, by confronting the power of evil, and by giving himself up to death as an example of the "Great Commandment." Such love, as Dorothy Day said, quoting Father Zossima in *The Brothers Karamazov*, "is a 'harsh and dreadful thing,' [where] our very faith in love has been tried through fire." Rather paradoxically then, what it means to be a Catholic today is expressed in few words and in profoundly simple teaching. When we repeat and live these, we are like the scribe, "not far from the kingdom of God."

PRAYING WITH SCRIPTURE

- Pray the words of Psalm 18, "I love you Lord, my strength," telling God in a simple way of your love.

- Think of someone you find difficult to love. Place yourself in his or her circumstances and love the person "as yourself."

- Pray about how you would present this gospel to someone who asks, "What does it mean to be a Catholic?"

Thirty-Second Sunday in Ordinary Time

Readings: 1 Kgs 17:10-16; Ps 146:7-10; Heb 9:24-28; Mark 12:38-44

"The fatherless and the widow he sustains" (Ps 146:9).

"You'll Never Walk Alone"—We Hope

As Mark's Jesus walks toward Jerusalem and his death, he comes across an assorted group of "little people" who embody Gospel values: a grieving father who cries, "I do believe, help my unbelief" (Mark 9:24); a bevy of children who remind him of what it means to enter God's kingdom; an unknown exorcist who casts out demons in Jesus' name; a blind beggar whose faith brings healing and who bounds up to follow Jesus. In today's gospel, which recounts Jesus' final public act before his farewell speech to the disciples and subsequent passion, a poor widow gives "her whole livelihood" (lit. "life"). She is a model of Jesus, who will shortly give his life for others. In the reading from the first book of Kings, a widow who has barely enough food for herself and her child, welcomes the prophet Elijah, only to be rewarded by God with an abundance of food.

In the ancient world, widowhood was a frightening prospect, as reflected in the frequent refrain in Israel's laws calling for special care for the widow, the orphan, the poor, and the stranger in the land. The Hebrew and Greek terms for "widow" come from roots that suggest helplessness, emptiness, or being forsaken, and what these people had in common was their isolation from the web of love and support, and a deep sense of powerlessness.

In traditional societies today a similar fate often awaits, crystallized in the statement of one such widow: "We are considered bad omens. We are excluded from all auspicious events. I am accused of being a witch who killed her husband, and my children were beaten and kicked out of our house by the brothers-in-law. We live by begging, in continual fear." In our seemingly prosperous society widows (and widowers) often suffer, in addition to their deep grief, economic loss, the burden of raising a family alone, and a strange isolation from friends, which often sets in soon after protestations of support at the funeral.

This gospel (in the longer form) is a two-edged sword. Jesus teaches in the Temple, which had recently been magnificently reconstructed by Herod, one of the great builders of the ancient world, a parade example of the "edifice complex" along with even nastier proclivities. The Temple area was twice as large as the Roman forum, and the sight caused Jesus' disciples to point to "the wonderful stones and wonderful buildings" (cf. Mark 13:1). It was a religious and commercial center with a large staff, requiring great financial resources.

After a number of disputes with the Temple establishment, Jesus lashes out at the scribes, pillorying their social and religious posturing —wearing elaborate vestments, glorying in signs of honor, but most harshly "devouring the houses of widows" by promising to recite lengthy prayers. (This sounds hauntingly like certain contemporary religious fund-raising techniques.) Jesus then sits, faces the treasury, and watches people donate money, most likely putting it in boxes marked "Alms," which have been found by archaeologists. A poor widow comes by; Jesus notices her as she throws in a couple of coins, the equivalent of a few pennies.

The contrast is stark, not only between the rich, who give out of their surplus, and the widow, but also between the widow and the scribes. In fact, many commentators argue that Jesus' statement that this poor widow put in all she had is not primarily praise of the woman but a prophetic indictment of the Temple establishment, who took advantage of such little people. In effect Jesus is saying: "Look at the way the scribes posture. This is what it all comes to— exploiting poor widows."

Yet Mark clearly focuses on the widow's deed. In contrast to the external signs of honor sought by the scribes, she possesses true honor in God's eyes. Her action not only symbolizes what Jesus will do but provides a "bookend" with the action of the woman in Mark 14:1-11, who with extravagant largess anoints Jesus for his death. These nameless "little people" are great in their courage and service, even in the face of powerful institutions that can exploit them and crush their loved ones. Their sisters are all around us today.

PRAYING WITH SCRIPTURE

- Pray for someone you know who has lost a spouse and think of ways you can ease that person's grief and isolation.

- Pray in gratitude for the many gifts that widows, widowers, and the unmarried bring to the Church today.

- Pray about ways that your parish or community might be more aware of the plight of widows and widowers worldwide.